*Christian
Meditation,
Its Art
and Practice*

CHRISTIAN MEDITATION, ITS ART AND PRACTICE

H. Wayne Pipkin

HAWTHORN BOOKS, INC.
Publishers/NEW YORK

CHRISTIAN MEDITATION, ITS ART AND PRACTICE

Copyright © 1977 by H. Wayne Pipkin. Copyright under International and Pan-American Copyright Conventions. All rights reserved, including the right to reproduce this book or portions thereof in any form, except for the inclusion of brief quotations in a review. All inquiries should be addressed to Hawthorn Books, Inc., 260 Madison Avenue, New York, New York 10016. This book was manufactured in the United States of America and published simultaneously in Canada by Prentice-Hall of Canada, Limited, 1870 Birchmount Road, Scarborough, Ontario.

Library of Congress Catalog Card Number: 76-19763

ISBN: 0-8015-1279-4

1 2 3 4 5 6 7 8 9 10

For Arlene,
of course

Contents

Foreword   ix

Preface   xi

PART I

Foundations

1   *The Search for Meaning in a Changing World*   3

2   *What is Meditation?*   13

3   *Christian Meditation*   23

PART II

Varieties

4   *A Christian Alternative to Trancendental Meditation*   35

5   *Dialogical Meditation: Prayer as a Two-way Conversation*   52

6   *Story Meditation: Exploring the Bible as a Participant*   80

7 *Intercessory Meditation: Participating with God in the Healing Process*   98

8 *Christian Meditation in a World of Action*   111

PART III

Resources

9 *Christian Meditation in the Local Church*   139

10 *What to Read*   146

Notes   161

Index   169

Foreword

There is an increasing hunger throughout Christianity for exploring the meditative state of consciousness for its spiritual value. Consequently, there is a very real need for leadership and literature regarding Christian forms of meditation. Tragically there has been a dearth of such help from within the Christian Church. In this book Dr. Pipkin makes a helpful contribution toward filling that void.

Dr. Pipkin's skills as a Church historian, showing how meditation fits in with the Christian roots, and as a small group leader encouraging growth through the use of meditation, provide a balance between the theoretical and the practical.

And speaking of balance, I am particularly supportive of Dr. Pipkin's balancing of the inner and outer aspects of the spiritual journey. Too often there has been a polarization, which has insisted that a person be either a contemplative *or* active in social justice. Any spiritual pilgrimage that looks to Jesus the Christ as a substantial clue, knows that it is *both*.

Wayne Pipkin is a friend and colleague who has written a very thorough and useful book. It is a pleasure to commend this book to the Christian who is serious about expanding his or her prayer life to include the meditative state of consciousness. There are increasing numbers who are experiencing the riches of that exploration.

L. Robert Keck, Director
New Wineskins Center
for Research and Development

Preface

The following book on Christian meditation is intended as an introduction to the varieties of meditation practiced by Christians. In our present time there are many alternatives calling for our attention and commitment. Misunderstanding has kept many Christians away from meditation. It was the recognition of this fact that led me to want to say that meditation is one of the disciplines which the ordinary Christian ought to be able to take advantage of in his or her daily Christian life.

My wife and I were first drawn into meditation by the story of Bob Keck and his work in the meditative prayer research project at First Community Church in Columbus, Ohio. As it happened, we were both interested in and drawn into the small meditative prayer groups at the church and found in the practice of meditative prayer a valuable and exciting mode of Christian experiencing. Soon we found ourselves leading a small group in our home and serving on advisory committees in the project.

As a church historian I began studying the role of Christian meditation in depth in the church's history. As a layperson I became greatly concerned that many Christians were unaware of the benefits which meditation could bestow. It was then that I became interested in writing an introduction to meditation for the average churchperson, in the hopes of dispelling the myths and fears that surround the practice of meditation. I am convinced that meditation is a very useful tool for the Christian, not the only one, but a very useful one.

The book is divided basically into three parts. The first part, chapters one through three, is introductory and foundational. It is an attempt to describe briefly the present situation in which we find ourselves at this point in American history. Within that broad cultural and historical context I next try to describe what meditation is and what specifically Christian meditation is. For the person who does not know what the basics of meditation are, the beginning is a good place to start. If, however, there is familiarity with the theory of what meditation is, then chapter four may be the place to begin. Chapters four through eight provide an analysis of the types of Christian meditation and offer some sample meditations. Chapters nine and ten are basically resource chapters for those wishing to explore the use of Christian meditation in the local church.

There are many persons to whom I am thankful for the role they have played in making this book possible. Many of the ideas were introduced to me by Bob Keck, and he has often encouraged me to delve further into the role of meditation in the church. All I can say is that I am grateful for his encouragement and affirmation.

Many of my former colleagues in the seminaries of Ohio have been helpful to me in large and small ways. Let me mention especially my appreciation for the hospitality and resources offered to me during the writing of this book by the Reverend Conan Taylor, OFM, dean of St. Leonard College in Centerville, Ohio, and the Reverend J. Raymond Favret, president of the Athanaeum of Ohio. They and their colleagues have contributed in a variety of ways to the formation of my thinking and the production of the book.

Several friends have been very kind in their assistance. Larry McGinty saw to it that I got the books I needed as soon as possible. Several friends read the second draft of the manuscript and made helpful suggestions: Barbara Dockter, Joe DeRosa, Pat Shuter, Marg Wells and Polly Swaney. Nancy-B. Blucher made it possible for an initial draft to be typed, and Edith Sotzing lent her support and expertise as the final lines were being composed. A sincere word of gratitude is offered for the assistance of these friends.

There are many others too numerous to mention who have played significant roles in the writing of the book, including scores of persons in a number of seminars and workshops.

The patience, creativity, joy in living, and constant support of my good friends and daughters Nancy Gail and Heather Michelle helped more than they knew. My best friend and wife, Arlene, has not only been my willing critic and partner in dialogue throughout the birthing of the book, it is she more than anyone who made it possible. Only she can know how grateful I am.

PART I
Foundations

1
The Search for Meaning in a Changing World

Every time period is known and experienced as having certain characteristics. Ours is no exception. We reach out to make sense of the age in which we live by describing our age and ages past as having some kind of unity. There was the Age of Faith, the Age of Reason, and the Age of Revolution.

How is our experience of the present day best characterized? Perhaps it is the Age of Anxiety. Others would suggest the Aquarian Age. Others the Age of Transiency.

A World of Change

The fact is, there is no unity as such today. There is only change. Change is our constant.

What we have today we will not have tomorrow. Where we live today we will not live tomorrow.

We are becoming or we have become an age without roots. Our seven-year-old daughter has lived in six different homes, two of which were known to be temporary at the time. Eight years ago, when I finished my academic work at Hartford, I fully intended to return to my native state of Texas and stay there for the next forty years. Today we live in Ohio and fully expect a major change in the near future.

It is the same everywhere. None of our friends in the small suburb of Worthington in which we live expect that their children will go to the schools they did, that they will have the same teachers, that they will even know the same places as anything more than a visitor.

Not long ago my wife and I went to a small birthday party at the home of a friend. The hostess prepared a parlor game, which the guests were to play so that we would be able to "get to know" each other. We had not known most of the persons there before that particular evening, and we likely would not be with them again in the future, even though we all attend the same church. The game we played illustrates the tenor of the present age. We were to make three columns on a page and list first that job for which we had been educated and trained. Second, we were to note what we presently did. Third, we were to list those things that we wanted to do. What struck us was how few of us were doing what we had been trained to do. We are being told that a person can expect to make on the average as many as three career changes during the course of a lifetime. That number will increase rather than decrease.

One of the more prophetic books to appear in recent years is Alvin Toffler's *Future Shock*. Toffler overwhelms the reader with the endless description of the changes that have and that are taking place in contemporary society. The change is of such a nature, he suggests, that many persons are simply refusing to admit that change even exists. We are somewhat like fish swimming around, blithely unaware that what we are swimming in is water.

Toffler suggests that the change that has overtaken us has reached epidemic proportions and that the omnipresent change issues in a feeling of dis-ease. He says:

Transience is the new "temporariness" in everyday life. It results in a mood, a feeling of impermanence. Philosophers and theologians, of course, have always been aware that man is ephemeral. In this grand sense, transience has always been a part of life. But today the feeling of impermanence is more acute and intimate. Thus Edward Albee's character, Jerry, in *The Zoo Story,* characterizes himself as a "permanent transient."[1]

Such transiency in its mildest form leads to discomfort. Today's change, however, is not mild, and the impact it is making on our lives, our society, our institutions, indeed on our psyche, is so great that the full significance of what is happening is not yet known.

Toffler describes the potential reaction as that of "future shock," a physiological and psychological reaction to rapid change not unlike what we have known as culture shock. Toffler warns that "there are discoverable limits to the amount of change that the human organism can absorb, and that by endlessly accelerating change without first determining these limits, we may submit masses of men to demands they simply cannot tolerate."[2]

Possible reactions include depression, anxiety, hostility to authority, apathy, and senseless violence. "Its victims often manifest erractic swings in interest and life styles, followed by an effort to 'crawl into their shells' through social, intellectual and emotional withdrawal. They feel continually 'bugged' or harrassed, and want desperately to reduce the number of decisions they must make."[3]

In essence it seems to me that this fact of transiency has produced a rootlessness and a feeling of homelessness in the world. How can you make yourself at home if you don't really know where it is you should call home?

The Abstract Society

Americans have been influenced for some time by the myth of the rugged individualist, the American ideal and folk hero. He emerges under many disguises. He is the Lone Ranger traveling around throughout the Old West, answering to none but the law above the law. If an American really wants to, he or she can go from log cabin, or peanut farm, to the White House.

It is part of the American myth that we are in charge of our own fate, that our government is responsible to our wishes. If we speak, we will be heard.

And yet there has arisen in recent years the growing awareness that we are, in fact, not in control of our fate, that those forces in society which determine how we will live out our lives are largely beyond our control. Society has, in effect, become an abstract society. We experience very concrete limitations on our freedom. This is, of course, understandable. However, if we try to influence society in a significant way, society itself seems to evaporate before our eyes. There just is not any easy way for the person today significantly to influence those forces that are exercising the most determinative kinds of influence.

We are not really the "captains of our fate." As sociologist Anton Zijderveld says, "The majority of society does not say "no" to this, but conforms and accepts its fate passively. In their increasing leisure time, these conformists withdraw into their own private world where they consume the commodities of an affluent society and the ready-made opinions of the mass media. The many complicated socio-political problems transcend their little worlds, are excluded from their lives."[4] As a result the majority of persons in society today are living in easy acquiescence with their powerlessness.

We have come to the point where we feel alienated from those bases of power that make the decisions in our society and in our world. We have particularly experienced over the last couple of decades a crisis of authority in our country. The vast majority do not have power, and those who do have, in effect, abdicated their roles of leadership. In recent years our political leaders in particular have become unbelievable.

No one who lived through Watergate could forget the utter disdain in which the leaders of our country held the people who had elected them. On the one hand we spoke of participatory democracy, and on the other our leaders decided what it was that we should and should not know. Language itself took on a strange character as we witnessed the debasing of words themselves. During the war we could hear a United States Air Force official say, "We had to destroy the village to save it."

It is not surprising that we have begun to wonder if we have not fallen into Alice's land on the other side of the looking glass, where things are not quite what they seem and where, in any event, we do not have the power to affect those forces that affect us.

The Age of Consumption

We have lost a sense of being at home in the world. We are no longer responsible citizens of an interrelated world. We have, in effect, turned toward material goods to satisfy our innermost longing. In effect, moral decay has set in.

We have developed a throwaway mentality, which utterly disregards the effect our consumption has on the environment. We hunt species to the point of extinction on the one hand and on the other consume natural resources as if they were renewable. Our obsessive attachment to the change that Toffler documents is having untold destructive effects on the ecosystem. John Taylor calls us the "waste-mongers."[5] What better term could be found for a people who each year discard 7 million cars, 48 million metal cans, 26 billion bottles, and 65 billion metal bottle caps?

We have reached a state where the only way of maintaining identity and filling the emptiness within is by acquiring new material goods. The measure of one's success is whether or not a new car or a color television set can be purchased. The irony is that we are not acquiring so that we can have. Acquisition has become an end in itself. Therefore, we go on acquiring more and more.

The fact is that such a style of acquisition is not satisfying. Who could believe for a moment that such a way of living was truly providing meaning for persons? And the worst part of it is that our ways of consuming have contributed to unrelieved poverty in the rest of the world. Although we compose only a small portion of the world's population, we consume the world's resources out of all proportion to our size. It is indeed questionable whether the world can go on supporting that small part of the world while the developing nations are kept in poverty. We have become victims of excess and consumption and are not responsible members of the human family. The problem with seeking meaning in consumption is that one's appetite is never satisfied. The void will never be filled. There will always be the need for more and more things to be consumed.

The Search for Meaning

There is deep within the human being the need to feel that life is worthwhile, that what one is doing gives meaning to life, that one's own particular life has meaning. It is this search for meaning in life which drives persons into self-defeating patterns of consumption.

We are engaged in a life-and-death struggle. Do our lives have meaning? Based upon the observations we have been making about life in the present age, is human existence best characterized by life or death? A few years ago Saul Bellow addressed himself to this question in his best seller, *Herzog*. At one point Bellow says, "But what is the philosophy of this generation? Not God is dead, that period was passed long ago. Perhaps it should be stated death is God. This generation thinks—and this is its thought of thoughts—that nothing faithful, vulnerable, fragile can be durable or have any true power. Death waits for these things as a cement floor waits for a dropping light bulb.''[6] Herzog's word is a despairing word. Our preoccupation with death, our shallowness of existence, our expertise in the creation and employment of weapons of destruction, our devaluing of human life make one wonder if Herzog is not right: Death is our God.

We have been too content to live the life of shallow existence. Life today too often at the personal level is empty, meaningless, and frightened. We see it in a woman losing herself in her work so that she becomes oblivious to those around her. We see it in the student lost in the drug scene, tripping from one high to another, looking for something to fill the void, to give meaning to one's particular life. We see it in the man losing himself in his religion so that he loses awareness of the real world.

The result of this frustrated attempt to find meaning is anxiety and alienation. We live in a society characterized by alienation. Individuals are alienated from that self they want to be, and they find themselves alienated, separated from others. We experience it throughout our country today. In our social life, even in our churches, people are alienated from one another, threatened or afraid of others for one reason or another.

There is an element missing in our lives, which forces us to be less than whole, which forces us to live a fragmented existence—a distortion of the true life that is available to us. This partial life can be characterized in many ways. One of the most biting characterizations of this half-life is that made by Charles G. Finney, Jr., the son of the famous evangelist in *The Circus of Dr. Lao*. He has Appollonius, the fortune teller, tell Mrs. Howard T. Cassan just how miserable her existence is:

> "Tomorrow will be like today, and day after tomorrow will be like the day before yesterday," said Apollonius, "I see your remaining days each as quiet, tedious, collections of hours. You will not travel anywhere. You will think no new thoughts. You will experience no new passions. Older you will become but not wiser. Stiffer but not more dignified. Childless you are, and childless you shall remain. Of

9

that suppleness you once commanded in your youth, of that strange simplicity which once attracted a few men to you, neither endures, nor shall you recapture any of them any more. People will talk to you and visit with you out of sentiment or pity, not because you have anything to offer them. Have you ever seen an old cornstalk turning brown, dying, but refusing to fall over, upon which stray birds light now and then, hardly remarking what it is they perch on? That is you. I cannot fathom your place in life's economy. A living thing should either create or destroy according to its capacity and caprice, but you, you do neither. You only live on dreaming of the nice things you would like to have happen to you but which never happen; and you wonder vaguely why the young lives about you which you occasionally chide for fancied impropriety never listen to you and seem to flee at your approach. When you die you will be buried and forgotten, and that is all. The morticians will enclose you in a worm-proof casket, thus sealing even unto eternity the clay of your uselessness. And for all the good and evil, creation or destruction, that your living might have accomplished, you might just as well never have lived at all.''

It is a bleak and despairing view, but one that is all too close to representing the fears of modern humanity.

A World of Options

Never has the search for meaning on the part of humans been more obvious, and never have there been more options vying for their consideration. There is a virtual plethora of alternatives available for the discriminating and nondiscriminating tastes.

Religion and religious offerings are available in the United States of the seventies in a bewildering offering of choices. Who could have guessed in the late sixties that the political activism of the protestors would turn to the inward searching of seekers? As the authors of one text in American religion note, "Not only is contemporary American religious belief and practice highly pluralistic, but it is at the same time a surprisingly vital and powerful force in American life. *Homo Religiosus*—man the religious animal—is alive and well in America."[8] It is a time in which there is a great variety, and the variety is bewildering. For many the variety is so vast as to be overwhelming, perhaps another sign of future shock.

As I was finishing the final pages of this book, the September 6, 1976, issue of *Newsweek* appeared with its feature story, "Getting Your Head Together." The variety of options available in the religious world now commands front-page attention. Americans are turning in unprecedented numbers to movements such as bioenergetics, psychosynthesis, TM, est, Rolfing, Arica and Silva Mind Control—to name only a few. "The consciousness revolution, once confined to the youthful counter-culture, has mushroomed into a mass movement particularly popular among the more affluent members of society who can afford the time and money to develop their inner depths. From yoga classes at the YWCA and university extension programs to local 'growth' centers and luxurious 'awareness' cruises in the Caribbean, the movement has created a network of therapeutic outlets servicing millions of Americans who are bored, dissatisfied with their lives or seeking a God they can experience for themselves."[9]

There is much in the variety of movements that is manipulative and lacking in taste, but there is much that is good in the overall growth of such movements. Theodore Roszak sees a genuine spiritual quest on the part of America and, furthermore, "that we can discern, through all these starry-eyed images of an Aquarian Age filled with wonders and well being, a transformation of human personality in progress which is of evolutionary proportions, a shift of consciousness fully as epoch-making as the appearance of speech or of the tool-making talents in our cultural repertory."[10]

What is certain is that the "consciousness revolution" reflects the search of modern humanity for a center, a place where they can focus. The modern movement reflects the human search for meaning, for freedom, and for a clearer perception of reality. Not

11

all the movements provide the answer, but we perhaps should take hope that once again modern humanity is taking the religious question seriously. The religious quest is recognized once again as an authentic search. In that certainly there is hope.

2
What Is Meditation?

The difficulties in writing about meditation are manifold. In the first place there are many different views as to what meditation is, dependent to a large degree upon which type of meditation is being practiced. In addition, the notion as to what meditation is has changed over the years so that there is much confusion as to what meditation is. Today, for example, a very limited view of what meditation is results from the overwhelming popularity of one particular type of meditation, namely, Transcendental Meditation.

Perhaps the greatest difficulty in writing about meditation, however, is that meditation should properly be experienced rather than described. As a general rule, human experiencing is so rich that when we try to use words to describe the meaning of the experience we lose something. The matter is complicated in the case of meditation when the experience is basically at a level in which words do not come into play, and therefore we are stuck with trying to use one mode of expression, words, to describe an experience that often uses a different mode of expression—symbols and feelings. Before describing what meditation is, then, it may be helpful to say a few words about the realm of human experiencing where meditation is of value.

Inner Being and Meditation

We Americans place a very high value on being rational and on being in control of our processes of thinking and acting. One of the most devasting statements we can make to a person is "You're being irrational!" We prize clear, logical, controlled thinking.

There is so much more to the human being than is encompassed in the rational and conscious way of being and doing. There is, in effect, another side of us, a side that is not wholly rational and not wholly subject to our conscious control. That side of us or part of us is called by many names. Some call it the "unconscious" or the "subconscious" or the "superconscious." Largely these are names given by particular schools of psychology and reflect their own views as to what is truly human. It is enough, however, to recognize that there is that side of our own experience over which we normally do not have conscious control.

There is a part of the human being that seems almost to have an independent existence. Every night we dream several times, whether or not we are aware of that fact. Some of us unconsciously suppress those dreams. Usually we just ignore them. What our dreams tell us, though, is that there is an enormous amount of experiencing that we as human beings are undergoing, over which we have little control and about which we are normally unaware.

The point I am trying to make about these things, without going into psychoanalytic theories with too great a depth, is that we as human beings have a marvelously creative part of our being, which we often do not pay attention to. There is more to us than the waking state. There is popular folk wisdom to the effect that when we have a problem to solve we can work on the problem by "sleeping on it." While we are asleep, our unconscious mind works on the particular problem, and often we will awaken with the answer. Furthermore, there are innumerable stories about inventors dreaming solutions to problems they were having with a particular invention.

The fact is, there is so much more to the amazing capacity of the human mind than is captured in our normal waking state of mind. How beneficial it would be if we could find ways to take advantage of this "other side" of our being and person.

Not only is there that part of us, which for convenience I am calling the unconscious, there is also a mode of consciousness that is very much a part of us as human beings but that we in the West have tended to suppress. I am referring to the intuitive, emotional, and feeling side of persons.

There has been some fascinating research in recent years into the functions of the two hemispheres of the brain, which tells us something about what it means to be a human being and how we in this country have tended to be content with less than the whole person. Robert Ornstein, in his insightful and stimulating book, *The Psychology of Consciousness,* describes the research that has taken place and draws several thought-provoking conclusions.[1]

The brain is divided into two hemispheres, the left and the right. We have known for some time that the left hemisphere controls the right side of the body and the right hemisphere the left. In addition, the two hemispheres have more specific responsibilities. The left side of the brain is the area which controls the verbal capacities of the human being. It is the rational and linear side. The right hemisphere, however, is the side of the brain which controls the intuitive and symbolic functions of the human being. Further, the right hemisphere maintains the visual and imaginative capacities of the brain.

Generally speaking, we have tended to exalt the functions of the left side of the brain. We even call it the major hemisphere. It is interesting to note that we have traditionally tended to look on left-handed people with some suspicion. A left-handed compliment is not a straight compliment. A helper is a "right-hand man." The examples could be multiplied. We have tended to exalt the person who utilized the left brain and tended to depreciate the person who utilized the right brain. In our culture, which has inordinately exalted the masculine side as the desirable side, we have sung with

Professor Higgins, "Why can't a woman be more like a man?" What we meant is that men are more rational. A woman is more emotional and feeling, and hence we have spoken with scorn of "woman's intuition." Fortunately, these prejudices are changing today, but the situation reveals how we have tended to place the rational, the linear, and the verbal as the more dominant and to-be-desired faculties in our society.

It is interesting to note that the research indicates that the two parts of the brain actually do specialize and that we do use different sides of the brain for different types of functioning. As interesting as that discovery is, however, it is of limited significance, for the fact is, the brain functions as a totality in normal functioning. That is, the communication between the two sides by means of the corpus collosum intends that the human being function as a whole and not as two parts. What is important is to recognize this, or we may end up dividing the human being in half.[2] The question is, why have we tended to repress the imaginative and creative side of the human being. The favor the brain and consciousness researchers have done for us is to remind us that the symbolic, emotional, visual and intuitive sides of reality are also distinctly human and therefore of value.

What we are confronted with is the recognition that there are valuable sides of human experiencing which we have tended not to make use of. We have let ourselves fall out of touch with our unconscious, and we have tended to depreciate the intuitive and feeling side of the human being. In doing, we are less than whole persons. Our goal, therefore, should be to integrate the parts of the human so that we become whole human beings and not partial persons.

States of Consciousness

Although we do not normally have or make access to our unconscious or to our intuitive side, we do make use of them on occasion. I have already suggested that we make regular use of the unconscious every night as we sleep. Daily we may often drift off into reverie and daydreaming when we become much more intuitive and visual in our experiencing. The times when we are doing this we are living in a different state of consciousness and awareness than we normally live in.

The ordinary state of consciousness (OSC) for most of us "is characterized by a high degree of rationality and a relatively low degree of imaging ability. We can usually think without making many mistakes in logic, and our imaginings usually contain mild sensory qualities, but they are far less intense than sensory perceptions."[3] As you are reading this book you are probably in the normal state of conscious awareness which we call OSC. The function of a state of consciousness is to allow us to cope with reality. The perceptions we have of what is "out there" are organized by our minds in certain ways so that we assign to reality an order that may not in fact exist. We simply become accustomed to what happens to us, and we are able to fit experiences into a general pattern.

One of the services that our state of consciousness performs for us is to filter out certain impressions. If we had to pay attention to every stimulus which came to us, we would simply overload after a while, and quite like an electrical circuit we would blow a fuse. Therefore, while you are reading these words you are not, strictly speaking, conscious of the lighting in the room, the noises inside and outside the room, the chair on which you are sitting, and other background sights and sounds which surround your vision and hearing. You are not aware of them until I mention them to you, and now you have no doubt enlarged your field of experiencing for a moment. The point is, if you were not able to relegate those kinds of experiences to another field than your conscious awareness, you would not be able to function for very long. This is a useful service. The problem comes when your conscious awareness inhibits those movements in your broader field of experience which would be of value to you.

We function so easily in the world we inhabit that we simply come to believe that we are seeing reality, that what we see and hear is what is really out there. There are many ways of illustrating this accepted premise, that we really organize and form what we call reality. It does not take very long for me to become aware of this when I walk in the woods or in the fields with my four-year-old Heather. We have often walked in the neighborhood of the Three Bears. Her world is full of magic, and although she is already well on her way to adjusting her world to that of the adult into which she will grow, she is not yet there. There is no such thing as a miracle for her because for her all things are possible.

An amusing incident reported by Karl Pribam illustrates the power of our assumptive world on our experiencing.[4] In a particular section of New York there was a train which used to run about eleven o'clock every night. The people in the neighborhood simply became accustomed to that noisy elevated train. Not long after the train was taken down, people in that neighborhood started "hearing things." The police reported that the neighbors started calling in quite regularly to report there were robberies and other assorted crimes taking place. What happened was the noise they had become accustomed to had been taken away, and the quiet was not yet assimilated into their ordinary conscious awareness. Therefore they were "hearing" something wrong. This is called the "Bowery El" effect and illustrates how our structured consciousness comes to operate in a certain way. The problem of the neighborhood was not that they were hearing anything, but that they were not-hearing something. The ordinary state of consciousness functions in much the same way and is, in essence, liable to the same weaknesses in interpreting what is seen and heard "out there."

One way to "take another look" at what is out there in the "real world" is to look from the vantage point of another or a different perspective. Such perspectives can often be gained by entering into an *altered state of consciousness* (ASC).

Much has been written about altered states in recent years.[5] It is not an especially difficult concept to grasp. An altered state is simply a state of consciousness which is different from a *baseline state of consciousness,* normally the OSC. When we sleep, we have entered into an altered state of consciousness. Hypnosis is also an example of an altered state, as is marijuana intoxication and drunkenness. Stanley Krippner identifies some twenty different altered states of consciousness.[6]

Without going into great depth, it is enough simply to say that in altered states of consciousness we experience external as well as internal reality in a different way. Krippner defines an altered conscious state as "a mental state which can be subjectively recognized by an individual (or by an objective observer of the individual) as representing a *difference* in psychological functioning from that individual's 'normal, alert, waking state.' "[7]

One should be cautious about suggesting that altered states are necessarily valuable in themselves, but it can be safely said that in an altered state one can obtain a fresh view of life and reality that can well be to the advantage of the individual. It is much like trying to gain perspective on a situation, only with much more force.

I would hasten to add that not all altered states of consciousness are of equal value and that not all of the altered states are to be sought. There is one altered state, however, that is of value, and that is the *meditative state of consciousness.*

The Meditative State of Consciousness

Meditation, then, is a state of consciousness that the individual can enter into consciously. In this altered or meditative state a person is able to enter into the realm normally known as the "unconscious." In addition, the meditative state is more at home in the right hemisphere of the brain and is therefore more intuitive, feeling and imaginative in its way of knowing.

Thomas Kelly writes, "Deep within us all there is an amazing inner sanctuary of the soul, a holy place, a Divine Center, a speaking Voice, to which we may continuously return. . . . It is a Light Within which illumines the face of God and casts new shadows and new glories upon the face of men. . . . The basic response of the soul to the Light is internal adoration and joy, thanksgiving and worship, self-surrender and listening.''[8] Kelly is writing about the unconscious wherein God speaks to humans and of the intuitive and feeling responses which humans make to the God who is within. The particular process which Kelly advocates in becoming responsive to God within is the process of "centering down." It is the approach of the meditator.

How does one enter into a meditative state of consciousness? One might first ask, how does one enter into an altered state of consciousness? Tart[9] points out that basically there is an induction process into an altered state which follows both disruption of the baseline state and patterning of the altered state. He gives going to sleep as an example. When we go to sleep we make ourselves comfortable, usually lying down and closing our eyes. By doing these things we disrupt our normal functioning and become unaware of the normal stimuli which would keep us awake. We add to this particular event tiredness or drowsiness which contribute to the disruptive forces. When we combine a sufficient number of the disruptive and patterning functions we fall asleep, incidentally not usually by trying to sleep, that is, if we adopt a passive attitude and "let go" then we will probably go to sleep.

Similar disruptive and patterning forces function in aiding the person's entrance into the meditative state of consciousness. "Most meditation techniques involve, as the initial step, sitting absolutely still in a posture that is not only comfortable, but that involves keeping the head, neck, and spine in a straight vertical line. A small but significant amount of muscular effort is needed to maintain this posture.''[10] The meditator reduces awareness of the body since his or her muscles do little more than maintain posture stabilization, thereby allowing the meditator to begin the movement into the meditative state of consciousness. Often, in fact, a beginning meditator will report that he or she became oblivious to the fact that he or she had a body.

Other patterning and disruptive forces in setting about to enter the meditative state include breathing exercises and concentration on a phrase or object. "This greatly restricts the variety of input to the system, inhibits thinking about various stimuli that come from scanning the environment, and in general takes attention/awareness energy away from, and reduces the activity of, the various subsystems of ordinary consciousness."[11] Thus by means of a variety of techniques, not unlike going to sleep, the meditator is able to enter into an altered state which we are calling the meditative state of consciousness.

Robert Ornstein describes basically two types of meditation from the psychological point of view. First there is concentrative meditation, the essence of which "seems to consist of an attempt to restrict awareness to a single, unchanging source of stimulation for a definite period of time. In many traditions the successful achievement of this is termed 'one-pointedness of mind.' "[12] A variety of meditative practices use this kind of meditation, including the mantra meditation used by both TM and various forms of Christian mysticism. As one recycles the same process over and over in the meditative state, one becomes unaware of external stimuli and the external world. Another way of speaking about this kind of meditation is to see it as "turning off" the bright light of the noonday and becoming aware of the stars which shine also at noon.[13] A second type of meditation according to Ornstein is the "Opening-Up Meditation" exercise. This meditation is also called in some disciplines "just sitting."[14] It is the most passive state of meditation and depends on the meditator just sitting in a meditative state, waiting for an opening up of awareness.

In general, then, meditation, whether it is "concentrative" or "opening-up," involves the shutting down of the normal chatter of the mind and the restriction of the awareness to one thing. The one thing may be a mantra, a fantasy trip, a leaf, or openness to a new awareness. The variety of possibilities for the Christian will be described below in chapters four through seven.

Benefits of Meditation

There are many benefits of meditation depending upon the particular school represented.

There are *physiological* benefits such as the reduction of stress and tension, thereby reducing high blood pressure.

There are *psychological* benefits such as increasing the ability to be open to new experiences as well as increasing the likelihood of self-knowledge.

There are *social* benefits resulting from the increased harmonious social relationships resulting from a calmer and more peaceful way of living.

For the Christian, however, these benefits are of a secondary nature. They are not to be put aside, of course. They are desirable and are not to be refused. The primary benefit for the Christian is the increased capacity for spiritual growth and practice. The Christian who practices Christian meditation will be able to benefit physiologically, psychologically, and socially from the practice of meditation. Meditation for the Christian is primarily to be used as a tool in the Christian life. The insight which comes is spiritual insight. What grows out of that insight is increased commitment and determination to live out the Christian life in the world.

3
Christian Meditation

Meditation is not necessarily Christian. Many non-Christian religions also make wise use of meditation. In fact, this obvious point is what turns many concerned Christians today away from meditation. It is too bad that this happens, because meditation has had a long history in the church and is one of many disciplines which can be helpful to the Christian.

We should understand that meditation is not *the* answer to what ails either the church or the average Christian. It is not the only tool which should appear in the Christian's tool kit. It is not even necessarily the best one. But it is a very good one, and one that too many Christians, particularly Protestant Christians, have tended to neglect. And so, although it is not the answer to every problem, Christians could increase their effectiveness as disciples if they were to become better aware of the nature and value of meditation.

Meditation is a human activity more than a specifically Christian activity. It is more a psychological and physiological process than a specifically religious one. From a strictly scientific point of view, when we meditate, we are engaged in the same practice as a Buddhist or a Hindu or a Sufi. The fact is, we all do a lot of things that are alike. Other religions have sacred writings and tell sacred stories. We don't therefore stop reading the Bible or refuse to listen to the Parables.

What is different in Christian meditation is not to be found in the process of meditation. What is different is the content and the context. The content is the Christian Gospel; the context is the Christian Church.

I am a Christian, professedly and unavoidably so. I have long ago learned that there is actually little I can do about that. I have been grasped by the reality of the love of God as revealed in Jesus the Christ, and it has so shaped the context of my life and the life of our family that it has become largely meaningless to think it could be otherwise.

Therefore what I am writing about and advocating is Christian meditation. I am not particularly concerned about the uniqueness of Christianity and whether what we have as Christians is different from or better than what others have. What I am concerned about is the sufficiency of Christianity and what is distinctively Christian. For that reason, now that we understand what meditation is, let us take a look at how meditation has been used in the church and what some of the underlying faith assertions might be on which a Christian meditator might build his or her practice of meditation.

Meditation in the Christian's Past

One of the distinctive facts of Christianity is that we are a historical religion. We not only have a history, somehow or other our faith itself is bound up in historical events. It therefore becomes very important for us to look back into our own history to see something of the use of meditation. A brief sketch is all that is possible, but it should be enough.[1]

Although we do not have explicit teachings on the subject in the Bible, meditative practices were not alien to the New Testament church. We could wish for a greater discussion on prayer in general and on meditation in particular, but as we'll see in chapter six, it is not the characteristic of the Bible to provide simple doctrinal lectures.

What we do see in the New Testament, however, is a context in which meditative practices were certainly used. John Killenger concludes, "I think it is important if we are to understand that the real power of prayer in Jesus' life came not from specific instances when he made requests for miracles, but from his whole life of meditation."[2] Understanding meditation as letting go, seeing differently and being receptive to the Presence of God is certainly not alien to the early church. We have tended to describe Jesus' life of prayer in magical terms, as we have his whole ministry. Killenger's further comment is worth reflecting on: "Jesus was not supporting a magical view of prayer. Instead, he was advocating the life of faith that comes from the discipline of prayerful meditation. The power in his own life came from such meditation. It seemed to emanate from his person wherever he went, so that the devils fell down and worshiped him. It did not come from localized, on-the-spot conjuring."[3]

When we take the trouble to look closely at the disciples in those early days as recorded in Acts what we do not see is a group running frantically about. We are told in Acts 1 that the disciples return to Jerusalem and wait. The early chapters in the church's history are stories of the followers of the Way remaining open to what it was that God had to tell them. It was a time of visions. When Ananias was praying, he was told to go to Saul of Tarsus. When Peter was praying in a trance, he saw a vision, after which he was told to go to Cornelius. When Paul was praying, he received the vision inviting him to Macedonia.

These kinds of experiences were meditative in nature. The early Christians had a lively meditative tradition in which they learned to wait on the Lord and to be receptive to his leading.

In much of the church's history a distinction has been made between meditation and contemplation, a distinction which is to a great extent lost today. Meditation was a more active form of observation on the Scriptures and on God's truth. Contemplation was often the stage that followed, that point at which God became the actor and the Christian was caught up by God. The distinction is not always this clear, and it is somewhat artificial. Nonetheless, as Louis Bouyer points out, the ancients recognized "a very clear distinction between meditation of the type then practiced and contemplation properly so called. And for them, without any doubt, contemplation was a state in which the soul somehow escaped from itself to be, as it were, ravished in God."[4]

There were some differences in the articulation of what meditation could achieve, but, generally speaking, meditation was understood as leading to a certain point, perhaps by meditating on the Scriptures and the recorded activity of God. Beyond that point contemplation "is supremely the gift of God: the especially privileged experience that we can have of His grace, of His very presence in us taking possession of us, and to that extent restoring us to the primal design of our creation to His image and likeness."[5] Contemplation, then, is basically that quiet form of waiting on God and remaining open to the leading which God offers.

Today the distinction between the arts of meditation and contemplation is somewhat blurred. In effect, we think of the two approaches as two sides of one coin, programmed and unprogrammed meditation. It is important to recognize that although we designate the two types of meditation, as Happold reminds us, "In practice they tend to intermingle. The meditating passes backward and forward from one to another; one may say that he engages in *mixed* contemplative prayer."[6]

Reflective and Imaginative Meditation

There are basically two approaches to active meditation. The one is the more rational and verbal, the other, symbolic and imaginative.

Peter of Alcantara, a sixteenth century Franciscan, described the two types of meditation in his *Treatise on Prayer*. In setting forth procedures which are to be followed by those who use his approach, he notes that after reading the appropriate passages of Scripture for the day or occasion, the meditation is to follow. His description of the two types of meditation is typical:

> There are some subjects which may be visualised by the imagination such as all the scenes in the Life and Passion of Christ, the last judgement, hell and heaven. Others pertain to the understanding than to the imagination—for example, the benefits of God, his goodness and mercy. . . . This kind of meditation is called *intellectual* and the other *imaginative*. We are wont, in these exercises, to use the one or the other, according as the subject-matter demands.[7]

It is striking that practitioners of Christian meditation anticipated the left brain/right brain research by several centuries!

The one type of meditation is of a reflective sort. It dwells on subject matter for which rational and verbal reflection is appropriate. Whether one took a particular passage of Scripture, a specific doctrine, or a thought-provoking passage from one of the Fathers of the church, one proceeds to move through the passage or doctrine in a verbal and rational way. This particular approach is not unlike what we usually encounter when we see a book of meditations or hear someone leading in a meditation.

The other type of meditation is more unusual, at least for those of us in the Protestant tradition. In the Catholic tradition there is a long history of this kind of meditation. It is, in fact, one of the major forms of meditation, known generally as the Ignatian method, after Ignatius of Loyola, who developed a lengthy series of imaginative exercises for use within a context of Christian devotion. The approach of Ignatius can be found in the devotional classic, *The Spiritual Exercises of St. Ignatius*.[8]

To use imaginative meditation, one actually visualizes the scenes chosen for the subject of the meditation.

> When the meditation is imaginative we must figure each detail as it
> actually exists, or actually happens, and must consider it as taking
> place in the very spot where we are, and in our presence. Such a
> representation will make our consideration and appreciation of the
> mystery more vivid. It will be even better to imagine all as taking
> place within our own hearts. If cities and kingdoms can find a place
> there, how much more a representation of these mysteries.[9]

By using the capacity for visualization, the meditator can actually
participate in the scenes in a way that rational reflection would not
allow.

The major problem with this kind of meditation is that it can
become so interesting in and of itself that it fails to serve the purpose for which it is intended. As in any good thing, too much is not
desirable. One could become so involved in the construction of
more and more elaborate fantasies that one has good entertainment
but not much spiritual growth. The process is interesting and
desirable, but one should avoid the extremes which become an end
in themselves, what Bouyer calls "picturesque but grossly con-
cretized imaginative representations."[10]

In approaching the imaginative meditation, one can approach
alone or with a guide, either as an observer or as a participant.
Morton Kelsey describes his approach:

> In approaching either a parable or an actual event, the secret is to
> become silent and concentrate on the picture or scene that is presented
> until it comes to life and begins to move. Then I find that there is a
> choice. I can stay on the outside and simply observe the action as it
> unfolds, or I can step onto the stage and become a part of the action. I
> can even become one of the characters, sometimes sharing in their
> joy, or often in their agony and pain and then in transformation and
> victory. It is amazing how the life of Jesus and the parables He told
> open up to reveal a living, growing meaning with us if we allow
> imagination to awaken them again and draw us into their reality.
> They speak at a deeper level than the intellect, touching the total per
> son as intellect seldom can.[11]

28

I cannot help but note that the point of our study and prayer life is not that we can understand at a distance what took place, but that we can understand within ourselves in a way that is decisively different for our daily lives. It is for this reason that Christian meditation becomes an intimately practical mode of learning.

Christian Faith and Meditation

As I suggested above, I come to meditation wearing Christian spectacles. I look at meditation from within a Christian context and am therefore somewhat colored in my assessment of it by my particular Christian point of view. By point of view I do not mean "opinion" but the understanding of life and reality which shapes and informs how I think, act, and make decisions. Since my own individual understanding of Christian faith will influence how I present Christian meditation as well as how I practice it, it is of some importance for what is to come that I set forth some of the faith principles which I see underlying the practice of Christian meditation. As I will present them here, they will be brief statements. The following chapters will more clearly explain and build on what is stated here.

For me the biblical understanding of God is a balance of a God who is not always seen as present and the God who is near. This is the balance between the transcendant God who is more than we are and the immanent God who is near to us, nearer to us than we are ourselves. To say that God is a living God is to recognize that God is also in process, as we are. To say that God is perfect does not mean that there is not movement and becoming within God. The Scriptures indicate that the existence of human beings makes a difference to God, that God actually cares for us. This intent to be together between God and the created order is part of the basis of meditation, for what God intends is communion between us and him.

29

God is still speaking to humans today. He did not stop speaking when the canon of the Bible was closed. Perhaps we stopped listening, but God did not stop speaking. This does not mean that God is changing his mind, but it does mean that there is the continuing possibility for God to speak anew and afresh in today's world. Meditation is not the only, but it is certainly one vehicle for that conversation.

God speaks through the historical, the truly human, the natural order. When we discover a human and natural means whereby God can speak to us, it does not have to be in itself specifically Christian, as meditation is not. The faith spectacles we wear as Christians, however, do not let us be impartial observers in the world, and therefore we see the possibility of God's speaking where others only see a physiological and psychological process. This should not be surprising. After all, even Jesus' disciples time and time again failed to see the Presence in their midst.

Part of the problem with us, however, is that we do not hear God speaking. Our minds and lives are so busy that we cannot hear the Word of God in our midst. It is for that reason that solitude is so important. If we stop what we are doing and return to silence, then we can perhaps shut down those distractions about us and hear God. This is the reason why we meditate, so that the prayer in which we are engaged can become a two-way conversation.

Not only is God continuing to speak, but God is saying certain kinds of things to us. Certainly one of the foundational affirmations for the Christian is the Incarnation, that God has somehow in a particular and individual life become human. In that act God has expressed approval for the authentically human life. Therefore, wherever God is acting to humanize persons, there we Christians ought also to be joining in. Meditation itself can contribute toward making persons whole and toward integrating the various parts of the human into a whole. We are rediscovering that we do not have souls so much as we *are* souls, that we do not have bodies so much as we *are* bodies. The Hebrew notion of the totality of the human is being rediscovered, and the whole of what goes into making us human can be fruitfully used.

There is a rhythm to the Christian life. We are both Mary and Martha, both quiet waiting and activity. But what is most important is not what we do, but who we are. For me that is the meaning of Grace, that we are accepted because God loves us as we are, not because we have in any sense earned the acceptance. However one chooses to live out the specific role given to him or her, it is to be lived out in the awareness of the Presence, indeed, in celebration of that Presence.

In the enchanting and thought-provoking story, *Mister God, This is Anna,* the anonymous author tells of one occasion in which the young child Anna noted that Fynn was playing with two copper circles, which were joined together like the links in a chain. He relates that

> Anna pointed to one of the circles and said, "I know what that is—that's me. And that's Mister God," she said, pointing to the other. "Mister God goes right through my middle and I go right through Mister God's middle."
> And that's how it was. Anna had grasped that her proper place was in God's middle and that God's proper place was in her middle.[12]

Such is the discovery that is potentially made in the practice of Christian meditation.

PART II
Varieties

4

A Christian Alternative to Transcendental Meditation

The rapid growth of Transcendental Meditation, or TM (a registered trademark), has been responsible more than any other single factor for the increased interest in meditation today. The phenomenal growth of TM centers throughout the country, indeed throughout the world, in which a fairly simple approach to meditation is taught at a fairly reasonable price has introduced meditation into the mass market in a surprising way. Whatever else one can say about the TM movement it certainly has been a business success, leading one pundit to call it "The MacDonalds of Meditationland."[1]

Transcendental Meditation

The man known as Maharishi Mahesh Yogi was born in the early part of this century in Central India. He no doubt grew up in the natural religious environment of the Hindu. His first professional training, however, was in physics, not religion. Nonetheless, he attached himself to a religious teacher, Swami Brahmananda

Saraswati, who was head of a mystic order in India. It was from this "Guru Dev" (Divine Teacher) that Maharishi learned what was to become Transcendental Meditation. After his teacher's death, Maharishi lived as a hermit for two years and then came out of solitude to start his movement. The first decade witnessed a gradual growth worldwide, reaching the United States in 1961 and England in 1962. The movement received a spectacular shot in the arm in the late sixties when celebrities like the Beatles and Mia Farrow became followers. A brief eclipse occurred at the end of the sixties. The mid-seventies have witnessed a spectacular growth of TM, which I for one believe is due less to the nature of the process of meditation than to the shrewd business mentality of the Maharishi. The Maharishi must have recognized at some time that for the majority of Americans to buy into something which was potentially so esoteric as TM he would have to sell it as a secular, non-religious product.

Transcendental Meditation is sold not as a religion but as a simple process, scientifically validated, which will provide all kinds of benefits for the person who tries it. One need not look far in any newspaper or bookstore to realize that the self-help product of whatever sort has a wide market. TM is in part riding the American predilection for easy self-improvement techniques. After all, who cannot afford forty minutes a day if it leads to lower blood pressure, lower tension, and sometimes to bliss?

The number of TM practitioners is large and is growing. There are well over 800,000 persons who have been initiated into the practice and there seems to be little sign that interest is declining.

Christian Responses to TM

The Christian response to TM has been mixed and understandably so. There are those who cannot ignore the obvious Eastern and Hindu trappings that accompany the process. The Christian opposition to TM runs the gamut from those who simply ignore what might be good in the process to those who are actively opposed. On some occasions the Maharishi has been picketed by Christian groups who see in the practice of TM an alternative religion to Christianity.

There are many Christians who do not see TM as an alternative religion to Christianity but as an aid to one's own Christianity. John R. Dilley, pastor of First United Presbyterian Church in Fairfield, Iowa, home of Maharishi International University, sees no essential conflict between his faith and the practice of TM. In fact, he argues that if anything TM has helped his faith.[2]

Dr. Una Kroll, M.D., an Anglican laywoman, has written in her book, *The Healing Potential of Transcendental Meditation,* that TM is a potentially helpful way of making Christian prayer even more meaningful.[3] For Christians who are concerned about the threat of TM to authentic Christian faith and practice, Dr. Kroll's book is worth reading. She is convinced that the similarities between Christian prayer and TM are greater than the differences, and that, in any event, it is not necessary to forego one's own Christian commitment in order to practice what she experiences as a helpful procedure.

The resistance to TM by many Christians reflects honest concern about what is appropriate for a Christian. Christians have generally long refused to dilute their commitment to Christ by engaging in non-Christ-centered religious practices. I personally think that the initiation ceremony which TM insists every practioner must go through before practicing TM is a religious ceremony. The elements of sacrifice and devotion to Guru Dev and the recitation of prayers to Hindu deities leave no other conclusion. For me, the question is not whether TM is in some sense a religious practice, but whether or not that practice will enhance or hinder the individual Christian's commitment to Christ. Only the individual person can answer that question.

It is unfortunate that TM has left such a negative image in the minds of many Christians. I have experienced resistance to specifically Christian meditation on occasion from Christians who were "turned off" beforehand by their understanding that all meditation must be Transcendental Meditation. One woman in our meditative prayer group which meets regularly in our home told us that her pastor simply cannot understand what she is doing. In fact, her pastor, she reports, took her husband to dinner to express his concern for what she was doing. No doubt the pastor is well-meaning, but he is also far off base. Not only is the practice of Christian meditation not a threat to her Christian faith, it has enriched her whole life and certainly enhanced her Christian experiencing.

On another occasion I did a short workshop at a nearby church on Christian meditation. Although the majority of the persons were most open and gracious to the presentations and were anxious to try out Christian meditation for themselves, there were those who spoke to the minister with some concern about me. I understand the concern, but it is misguided. There simply is very little connection between Christian meditation in its variety of approaches and TM, but the fear of TM has caused many Christians to be inordinately afraid of anything that looks something like TM. Unfortunately, many Christians have a tendency to "throw out the baby with the bathwater."

The Practice of Transcendental Meditation

The essence of Transcendental Meditation involves the use of a mantra, a simple Sanskrit word given to the practitioner at the time of initiation. For Americans the word is essentially a nonsense word, since Sanskrit is unfamiliar. Americans usually do not know what the word means, thereby increasing the simplicity of the task. There is no temptation to become involved in reflecting on the meaning of the word and hence to become distracted. The mantra, specially chosen from a small pool of words, is given to each person based upon certain criteria related to the station and personality of the person. The criteria for making the choice are known only to the TM instructors. When the mantra is given, the participant must promise never to reveal it. Supposedly, the mantra would not work if it were not a secret.

There are numerous descriptions of the TM initiation and practice to which the reader may refer if there is interest in what exactly takes place during the practice of TM.[4] In general, the meditator is told to sit comfortably and to say the mantra over and over silently. The meditator is not to try to concentrate too hard but is to let the mantra flow through the consciousness. If one becomes aware that the mind is wandering, one should return gently to the mantra. Certainly one should not become upset or try too hard. Rather, one lets go of the normal functioning of the mind and allows the consciousness to be drawn deeper and deeper into oneself. The meditation is to be practiced twice daily for approximately twenty minutes at a time. The meditation should be done before breakfast and dinner rather than just after, and one should generally avoid meditating late in the evening. The energy which results from the deep meditative experience may very likely prevent a person from sleeping.

The genius of Transcendental Meditation is its simplicity. Another admirable quality is the follow-up possibilities which can be utilized. If the meditator has difficulties, there are opportunities to return to the training center to have a specially trained teacher discern what the problems are and to make the necessary adjustments in the meditator's approach. There are also numerous continuing educational events to which the meditator can go for further training in the Science of Creative Intelligence, as it is called.

A Secular Alternative to TM

During 1975 a secular alternative to TM emerged in the work of Dr. Herbert Benson, M.D. Offered as a method of treatment which "takes the nonsense out of meditation," *The Relaxation Response* became a best seller.[5] Dr. Benson is currently associate professor of medicine at the Harvard Medical School and director of the Hypertension Section of Boston's Beth Israel Hospital. He was specifically interested in the problems of hypertension, or high blood pressure, a malady which affects all too many Americans. He became aware that TM was being touted as one solution to the problems of modern-day living. He investigated the use of TM, beginning in 1968 together with Keith Wallace, at that time a Ph.D. candidate in physiology at UCLA.[6] Certain beneficial physiologic changes appeared in the subjects studied such as lowered oxygen consumption, heart rate, respiration and blood lactate—all indicators of decreased activity of the sympathetic nervous system and indicative of a definite restful state.

The conclusion which Benson reached was interesting and suggestive: persons who meditated regularly were indeed less open to diseases of stress and clearly benefitted from the practice of meditation. Benson came to the conclusion that whatever was happening was opposite to the "fight-or-flight" response in which "humans, like other animals, react in a predictable way to acute and chronic stressful situations, which trigger an inborn response that has been part of our physiologic makeup for perhaps millions of years."[7] Benson concluded that we humans call all too often upon this fight-or-flight response. For this reason we are witnessing an epidemic of stress-related diseases in this country. Meditation was clearly, then, one possible response to this epidemic. Further investigation by Benson, however, led him to conclude that although certainly practitioners of Transcendental Meditation were able to reduce the destructive effects of stress by their meditating, it was because they were able to marshal the benefits of another human capability which was contrary to the fight-or-flight response. He concluded that "each of us possesses a natural and innate protective mechanism against 'overstress,' which allows us to turn off harmful bodily effects, to counter the effects of the fight-or-flight response. This response against 'overstress' brings on bodily changes that decrease heart rate, lower metabolism, decrease the rate of breathing, and bring the body back into what is probably a healthier balance. This is the Relaxation Response.''[8] He further concluded that this Relaxation Response was available to persons who were not practicing TM; that is, the technique could well be used without going through the trappings of the TM movement itself, including the initiation and the $125 fee.

Understandably the devotees of Transcendental Meditation were horrified. Now it was being suggested, and apparently believed by those who were buying the book, that anyone could achieve the benefits of TM merely by reading *The Relaxation Response*. The TM response was vigorous and a bit ridiculous. It was suggested that, like open-heart surgery, TM could not be self-taught, and that grave dangers awaited those who tried to practice TM without the guidance of the certified instructor. Since the evidence does not bear out the true believers of TM, one wonders if it is not the initial fee more than the certified instructor which is the major item of concern. The fact is, when the TM forces chose to market their product in terms of its medical and physiological benefits and offered it as the product of the "Science of Creative Intelligence," they were leaving themselves open to the creative research of a Herbert Benson. As I will suggest later the main reasons for practicing mantra meditation are not the physiologic benefits, though these are not to be denigrated.

The steps to achieving the Relaxation Response as given by Benson are simple. First, a quiet environment is to be used, preferably one which is calm, quiet and with very few distractions. When there is a quiet environment, it is easier to practice the response since distracting thoughts will not interfere. Secondly, a "mental device" is to be sought. "To shift the mind from logical, externally oriented thought, there should be a constant stimulus: a sound, a word, a phrase repeated silently or aloud; or fixed gazing at an object.''[9] If one is saying the word, the eyes are usually closed; if gazing, of course the eyes are open. The use of the word or object limits the distractions and increases the possibility of the response being elicited. The third component is a passive attitude. Above all one should not become concerned with how well one is doing. If one is seeking a *relaxation* response it becomes self-defeating to worry when thoughts slip into the meditation. "The passive attitude is perhaps the most important element in eliciting the Relaxation Response. Distracting thoughts will occur. Do not worry about them. When these thoughts do present themselves and you become aware of them, simply return to the repetition of the mental device."[10] Wandering thoughts are to be expected, and this warning defuses any undue worrying which could conceivably result from the desire to do a good job in the meditation. The fourth component is a comfortable position. The purpose of the posture is to reduce muscle tension. Understandably, one should not be so comfortable that sleep ensues.

If a person practices the technique outlined above, he or she will undoubtedly elicit the Relaxation Response and will achieve certain benefits such as relieving the stress which leads to high blood pressure, hardening of the arteries, heart attack and stroke. Other possible benefits include reducing the tendency to smoke, drink, and use drugs. The Relaxation Response reputedly helps persons sleep while at the same time conserving the body's store of energy, and allows persons to become more alert so that they can focus on what is really important. These benefits themselves surely warrant a serious consideration by anyone who wishes to live a full and meaningful life. For the Christian, however, there are other reasons to practice meditation with the help of a mantra.

A Christian Alternative to Transcendental Meditation

There are many examples of Christian types of meditation and prayer which make use of a mantra, and it must be said that the purpose of using the mantra in the Christian context is not for the physiological but the spiritual benefits which follow. Although it is relatively simple to select and use a mantra, the kind of meditation which appropriates a mantra is not, as John White in is little paperback, *Everything You Want to Know about TM Including How to Do It,* suggests, merely an introductory type of meditation.[11] In the Christian tradition the mantra is used in contemplative meditation and may well be considered the highest form of Christian prayer and meditation. Generally speaking, the mantra type of meditation has not been emphasized very much in Western Christianity.

In Christian practice a mantra is a word or a phrase which is used in contemplative prayer. As distinct from TM, the word or phrase is a meaningful one. It was thought that certain words by their very sound would have a particular kind of effect on people, much as certain musical instruments and kinds of music have that effect. We do not even know the origins of certain mantras which have long been used in the church. The spiritual exercises which use these mantras are "definitely designed to cultivate increased sensitivity to different sounds."[12]

One of the most quoted sources in Christian literature today on the mantra comes from the fourteenth-century writing, "The Cloud of Unknowing." An anonymous English monk, the author writes:

> If you want to gather all your desire into one simple word that the mind can easily retain, choose a short word rather than a long one. A one-syllable word such as "God" or "love" is best. But choose one that is meaningful to you. Then fix it in your mind so that it will remain there come what may. This word will be your defense in conflict and in peace. Use it to beat upon the cloud of darkness above you and to subdue all distractions, consigning them to the *cloud of forgetting* beneath you. Should some thought go on annoying you demanding to know what you are doing, answer with this one word alone. If your mind begins to intellectualize over the meaning and connotations of this little word, remind yourself that its value lies in its simplicity. Do this and I assure you these thoughts will vanish. Why? Because you have refused to develop them with arguing.[13]

This passage is not only suggestive in giving a mantra for the Christian to use, it is also helpful in noting the procedure and method which is used in the mantra meditation. It bears further looking at.

First, a simple mantra is to be chosen. A complicated mantra might provide more problems than help. One can become so attached to saying the words or sentences without making a mistake that the mantra becomes an end in itself; therefore, a simple mantra is preferable. The monk makes it clear that a meaningful mantra is to be chosen. The word or words should be said silently in the mind, without trying too hard.

The writer's reference to the Cloud of Forgetting is merely a description of what happens when the mantra is being said in meditation. One simply normally becomes unaware of anything except for the possible exception of the mantra; hence, the Cloud of Forgetting is entered. Psychologically, this is a typical experience reported by persons entering an altered state of consciousness. The advice on distractions is also similar to contemporary meditation approaches: "Should some thought go on annoying you demanding to know what you are doing, answer with this one word alone." That is, while one is meditating with the mantra, one does not engage in rational reflection; rather, one simply repeats the mantra. If it should happen that distractions arise, they are not to be addressed at the time. Instead, they are to be answered with this one word.

What the author of the treatise is seeking is simply the awareness of the presence of God. It is for this that the mantra is used. It is not an end in itself. Rather, God is the end. What one achieves by means of the mantra is entrance into The Cloud of Unknowing. This does not mean not-knowing, but un-knowing. The language is a bit strange to our ears but what he means is that by means of saying the mantra in the attitude of prayer one comes simply to experience God, to love God, to be aware of God.

Elsewhere the monk writes, "Contemplatives rarely pray in words but if they do, their words are few. The fewer the better, as a matter of fact; yes, and a word of one syllable is more suited to the spiritual nature of this work than longer ones.''[14] It is not unusual to discover while saying the mantra that the mental device slips away. The state in which one then rests is variously described. In TM it is called the Fourth State of Consciousness. In Christian terms it is understood as being aware of the Presence of God. It is a state which comes upon the meditator as a surprise and it is therefore most often understood as a result of the Divine initiative. It is the moment in which the seeker rests most closely in the hands of God. The notion of gift is often expressed at this point. For although the seeker works very hard to find God by means of the contemplative approach it is understood that it is God who makes the journey possible; indeed, it is God who instills the desire to make the journey. "Contemplative prayer is God's gift, wholly gratuitous. No one can earn it."[15]

The Way of the Pilgrim

Another type of contemplative prayer which uses a mantra originated in the East and is currently receiving wide attention in the West. Known technically as hesychasm, it is a spiritual exercise which uses the so-called Jesus Prayer. There is much material on the Jesus Prayer available in English, including a selection from a five-volume set of writings entitled the *Philokalia*. The currently most popular treatment of the Jesus Prayer is found in "The Way of a Pilgrim," written by another anonymous Christian.[16] The story is that of a nineteenth century Russian pilgrim who travels throughout Russia and Siberia. The work is a devotional classic and is worthy of being read by anyone interested in the history of Christian devotion or in the variety of ways to practice meditation and prayer.

The pilgrim narrates the story. He is searching for the meanings of the words of Paul to the Thessalonians: "Pray without ceasing.'' He travels from teacher to teacher until he finds one who tells him that the meaning of the words can be understood as an admonition to pray the Jesus Prayer, "Lord Jesus Christ, have mercy upon me.'' He is told to pray the prayer at first 3,000 times a day and then 6,000 and then 12,000 and finally as many times a day as he wishes. The major part of the book details his travels as he goes from place to place, saying the prayer and testifying to its value and power. He writes that the ceaseless repetition of the prayer has made all people of value to him: "During the day if I happened to meet anyone, all men without exception were as dear to me as if they had been my nearest relative.''[17]

The prayer became second nature to the pilgrim:

> Now I did not walk along as before, filled with care. The calling upon the Name of Jesus Christ gladdened my way. Everybody was kind to me, it was as though everyone loved me. . . . And that is how I go about now, and ceaselessly repeat the Prayer of Jesus, which is more precious and sweet to me than anything in the world. At times I do as much as forty-three or four miles a day, and do not feel that I am walking at all. I am aware only of the fact that I am saying my Prayer. When the bitter cold pierces me, I begin to say my Prayer more earnestly and quickly get warm all over. When hunger begins to overcome me, I call more often on the Names of Jesus, and I forget my wish for food. When I fall ill and get rheumatism in my back and legs, I fix my thoughts on the Prayer and do not notice the pain. If anyone harms me I have only to think, "How sweet is the Prayer of Jesus!'' and the injury and the anger alike pass away and I forget it all.[18]

The prayer is to be said methodically, perhaps dividing it on the inhalation and expiration of the breath, or perhaps in cadence with the heart beat. The methodical method is not unimportant, but it is not to be an end in itself. It seems to me that the method is simply to guarantee the induction into an altered state of consciousness in order to allow the prayer to flow through the depths of the human consciousness.

The hesychastic prayer is an obvious prayer for use in the time of personal and private devotion and prayer, although it does have communal overtones which emerged in the *Kyrie Eleison, Christe Eleison, Kyrie Eleison*. It can be said as part of one's personal prayer both morning and evening, or it can be used at other times. The form of the prayer has variations. One might insert the words "Son of God" between the phrases, and one might also add the words "a sinner" at the end. I personally use the phrase "Lord Jesus Christ, Son of God, have mercy on me" when I use the hesychastic method. I will no doubt experiment with other mantras later, but at the present time I have not yet exhausted or been exhausted by this particular one.

Selecting a Christian Mantra

There are many other mantras which can be used. Herbert Benson simply recommends using the word "One." He had endeavored to get away from words with religious meaning, but he has chosen a word which has rich religious overtones and even underscores the nature of the experience which results from this type of meditation, that is, at-one-ment, or atonement.

Some Christians use the Lord's Prayer as a mantra. It would be difficult for me to do so, since the meaning of the prayer would inevitably keep entering my consciousness. If it works, however, then I see no reason why it could not be suitable. The rosary has been a mantra for many Christians, both Roman Catholic and Protestant. Carlo Carretto writes of the value of prayer with a mantra by saying that at the beginning in prayer words begin to pour out, but that "in the end they are reduced to some monosyllable which none the less contains everything."[19] He speaks of the mantra prayer as the Prayer of Simplicity, the prayer which is to be used "when words are superfluous and meditation is difficult, almost impossible."[20] Carretto writes of the words which are poor words, but rich in content: "Hail Mary . . . Hail Mary . . . Jesus I love you . . . Lord have mercy on me . . . My God and my all. . . . It is strange how in these ejaculations, monotonous and simple, the soul finds itself at ease, almost cradled in God's arms."[21]

The variety of mantras is as endless as Christian experiencing is diverse. Francis of Assisi, who prayed for hours on end, was discovered by a companion on one occasion simply repeating the word, "Jesu, Jesu, Jesu." For Francis the name of Jesus was his mantra. In the meditation group which meets in our home one person chose the mantra, "Friend and love." Another chose the word, "Yellow," a creative expression of a very personal sort. Another possible mantra, it would seem, would be the affirmation "Yes." In one workshop one of the participants testified to her mantra. She said that she used the words, "Praise God." The experience she reports as being quite phenomenal. On one occasion she experienced a flooding of light. In general it has become an occasion of deep worshipfulness. She does not use her mantra lightly because it is at that time she feels very intensely in touch with God. She also recounts that after her meditation of this sort she receives a surplus of energy. It is an overwhelming experience. This, I think, points in the direction we want to go in using the mantra. The physiologic benefits, again are not to be denigrated, but for the Christian there is also the intention of worship. "The soul wants to remain still, directed towards God alone. It desires inner peace, quiet and repose; it no longer feels the need to use the human faculties."[22] It is indeed a time of great rest. It is rest which recreates and enlivens. It is an experience which suggests the fresh winds of the Spirit blowing through the soul, cleaning out the weariness and distractions.

Meditation: The Prayer of the Heart

PURPOSE

To select a mantra and to practice contemplative meditation with the selected mantra.

PROCEDURE

Select one of the mantras which has been described in the chapter above or choose a word or phrase which will be meaningful for you. Should you prefer not to use a word/phrase which has meaning you might prefer merely to count your breaths. I recommend that you count up to four and start over. Count only on the expiration of the breath beginning with one.

Find a quiet, comfortable place to sit or lie. The danger in lying down is that you might go to sleep. Perhaps the best position is sitting comfortably in a straight-backed chair. Some prefer to sit on a cushion on the floor or on a carpet. If necessary for comfort, loosen whatever clothes are constricting you. You might want to take your shoes off and set them aside.

Begin with a few deep breaths and then do a relaxation exercise. Imagine in your mind's eye that you are becoming progressively relaxed with each breath, until you have come from toe to head.

THE MEDITATION

Begin to voice silently your mantra, finding whatever rhythm requires the least effort. Do not fight it. Let the word/phrase have its own life. If it is one word, try saying the mantra on the expiration of your breath. If it is a longer phrase, divide the "voicing" of it between the breathing in and out. Do not worry if other thoughts come into your mind, but know that you can deal with any thoughts at a later time. Whenever you become aware of distracting thoughts merely return to your mantra.

You will not want to end your meditation suddenly. Set a clock where you can see the face. When you begin take the phone off the hook, or better, cover it with a pillow. You will want to spend about fifteen or twenty minutes in your meditation. When you check the time, if it has not yet been fifteen minutes, return to your meditation. If the time has passed, then begin slowly to return to the normal level of consciousness. Do so by becoming aware of feeling returning to the various parts of your body. Begin stretching your limbs and taking a few conscious deep breaths. You will soon discover what is the best way to return to normal awareness. Some do not like to return too quickly; others see no point in taking a long time.

DEBRIEFING

If you think you went to sleep during the meditation, perhaps you did. You may also have experienced that deep awareness of God's presence which is pre-symbolic awareness. If you feel you went to sleep, you might want to continue your meditation for another ten minutes, or you might simply set it aside for another day. Rest is good and if you had a short nap, you ought not worry about it. In fact, let yourself enjoy it. Your unconscious was not asleep, and it was able to take advantage of the time. Perhaps certain thoughts, images and symbols came to your mind while you were in the meditation. Now you can deal with them in whatever fashion is appropriate. Perhaps you might ask yourself why they came at this particular time. Often when you enter into the meditative state, you are "shutting down" the mind chatter which normally distracts you and you might allow some important thoughts and concerns which have been trying to get through to you finally to make their way in. Do not disregard them after you have done your meditation. You might discover something of significance. You might also frankly discover that the thoughts and images were only an attempt to keep you from entering into the meditative state. Resistance is not uncommon.

If you had an experience which was of some significance for you, I would suggest that you counsel with a trusted friend about it. Although you carry out this time by yourself in solitude, you will want to test out your experiences in the context of the Christian community.

VARIATIONS

You might choose to try the mantra meditation on a daily basis, in the morning and afternoon. Remember that you will have limited success if you do it after a meal. You will do no damage, but since the digestion of your food is underway, you will likely go to sleep. You might want to vary your mantra. Perhaps you will stick with the one that you have. In any event, you will want to feel free to make changes when appropriate. One possible variation might be to use the contemplative meditation within the context of your normal prayer time. Perhaps you will want to begin with the meditation, or to follow your normal reading of psalms, scripture and expressing of prayers by entering into the contemplative state. There are many different elements to prayer and praise. You do not need to limit yourself to any particular one. My own particular style of personal worship is to have the meditation time separate from the normal personal devotion time. For me this is a way of enhancing the movement toward prayer without ceasing.

5
Dialogical Meditation: Prayer as a Two-way Conversation

Most prayer is a one-way conversation between us and God. I don't think it was meant to be that way, but it seems that mostly we are addressing our petitions and concerns to God when we are praying. It's almost as if we assume that God would or could not know what was going on if he didn't have this hotline from his agents in the world to keep him aware of what's happening. That idea of course is amusing to the point of distraction. How absurd that God would need us to tell him about what's going on, and yet how much of our prayer seems to be that way.

The other feature about our prayers is the unvoiced assumption that God doesn't have anything to say to us, that we have already heard everything that God wants to say. Now, I don't think we would say it so boldly, but most of our prayers are saying just that. Meditation, however, can be a way of restoring the dialogue to prayer, of turning the one-way address into a two-way conversation.

One of the problems in any conversation is that we just don't listen. Normally we are so engaged in our own line of reasoning, what we want to say next, how we will follow up on what is being said in the conversation about us, that we just don't listen. How many times have we noticed in our own conversations with another person that they just didn't really seem to hear what was being said? Could others have noticed that about our conversation too? All too often we are just too distracted by what is going on in our own heads in the midst of a discussion that we really do not listen.

Time is another problem. We just don't have enough of it and it is so hard to take time to hear what another person is saying. And yet, it's not that we don't have time; it's that we don't take time.

We lose so much by not listening. Michel Quoist drives this point home to me everytime I read his prayer entitled, "The Telephone":

> I have just hung up; why did he telephone?
> I don't know. . . . Oh! I get it. . . .
>
> I talked a lot and listened very little.
>
> Forgive me, Lord; it was a monologue and not a dialogue.
> I explained my idea and did not get his;
> Since I didn't listen, I learned nothing,
> Since I didn't listen, I didn't help,
> Since I didn't listen, we didn't commune.
>
> Forgive me, Lord, for we were connected,
> And now we are cut off.[1]

If it is that way in our conversations over a telephone, how much more significant is it in our conversations with God, where we all too often talk but do not listen, and therefore do not learn—do not commune.

Dialogue with God in the Bible

The Scriptures are full of stories which suggest that God has a lot to say to people. Time and time again there are stories told where God is in intimate conversation with a human being. The biblical view certainly is not that God does not have anything to say. The question is, do we listen?

In the Old Testament the prophets are often depicted as involved in running conversations with God. Jeremiah was one such prophet. At the beginning of his writing, the prophet writes, "The word of the Lord came to me: 'Before I formed you in the womb I knew you for my own; before you were born I consecrated you, I appointed you a prophet to the nations.' " (Jeremiah 1:4-5)

The picture is that of a conversation in which God says to the prophet that even before his birth God had designs on his life and had in fact chosen him. Whether it was a real conversation, I don't know. What I rather think happened is that Jeremiah at some point had stopped what he was doing long enough to look back over his life and see that God was in fact involved in it in an intimate way that could only be described by affirming that God had chosen him, that all of his life had gone into making him into a prophet, and that this only made sense when he realized that God had called him, had in fact chosen him.

The notion of the call was necessary to Jeremiah's ministry, and it came most clearly to him when he was quiet enough to "hear" God saying to him, "Before I formed you in the womb I knew you for my own." Jeremiah describes the experience only by saying that "The word of the Lord came to me." What I think is probably different in the prophets of the Old Testament, that is, different from us today, is not that the word of the Lord came to them, that God spoke to them, but that they *heard* what God was saying to them. It was that fact which made all the difference.

Often the report is that God spoke, or that the "Word of the Lord" came to the prophet. God also spoke to the prophets in other ways, and it also took a certain amount of listening to be able to discern what God was saying. And although we are in a sense "reading between the lines" as we look at these experiences, I don't think we are doing an injustice to the intent of the Scripture or, more importantly, to the message by suggesting that one reason the prophets heard God and discerned the message was not because God forced his message on them, but because God's prophets were sensitive enough to stop, to see, and to hear God's message.

The conversation between God and Jeremiah related in the first chapter continues with Jeremiah hearing a message from God while looking at an almond in bloom: "The word of the Lord came to me: 'What is it that you see, Jeremiah?' 'An almond in early bloom,' I answered. 'You are right,' said the Lord to me, 'for I am early on the watch to carry out my purpose.' "(Jer. 1:11–12)

This particular passage has fascinated me for a long time. With a little imagination I can reconstruct what could well have taken place. It was a crucial time in Judah's history. The religious practices had become shallow and perfunctory. There was a plethora of gods, as many as there were cities (Jeremiah 2:28). The Children of Israel had turned away from their God to idols, crying "You are our Father" to a block of wood and "Mother" to a stone. (Jeremiah 2:27) They had brought themselves dangerously close to the brink of destruction. The northern kingdom, Israel, had in fact already fallen. The images Jeremiah uses are at once poetic and overwhelming:

> Two sins have my people committed:
> they have forsaken me,
> a spring of living water,
> and they have hewn out for themselves cisterns,
> cracked cisterns that can hold no water. (Jer. 2:13)

With this very sad situation much on his mind, certainly Jeremiah must have become aware of the impending doom. For one thing, if Judah did not have the strength which comes from rallying together as one people around the one God who had brought them out of Egypt they were particularly vulnerable.

On some occasion I think Jeremiah must have been outdoors,

walking along, as his eyes spotted an almond tree which was known as the "waker tree." The tree was called that because it broke into blossom even before its leaves were opened. Judah had just passed through a difficult time when the evil king Manasseh had reigned. Everywhere Yahweh seemed to be quiet and not acting, but now suddenly Jeremiah saw the almond tree and made a marvelous play on words. The Hebrew word for the almond was *shaqed.* As Jeremiah let his mind wander to the *shaqed,* the word *shoqed* leapt into his mind. The message from Yahweh came home: Yahweh is on the watch *(shoqed)* and although he may seem to be quiescent, like the blossoming almond tree *(shaqed)* he is about to burst forth alive.

The Jeremiah experience is a paradigm of God's speaking to the person who listens. How many people had passed that almond tree, and how many had missed seeing any possible significance for the present time in that simple, yet profound act of nature? Jeremiah passed it and the message came. I don't think Jeremiah went out looking for an almond tree to give him a message from God. The point is, he was receptive to it when it presented itself.

It is the same way in dialogical meditation. We allow God to speak to us. Prayer then becomes a two-way conversation. It is not that God is not speaking, that his truth is not any longer available to us. The fact is, as Samuel Miller writes, God's truth "is just as available as any other truth and only requires a man's individual attention and responsibility to be accepted. In fact, God is more available to men than the daily newspaper or the radio if they are only willing to pay attention to their own existence."[2]

Although we would not say that we believed it, it seems to me that most of us Christians live our lives as if God had stopped speaking to humanity when the Bible was written and the canon was closed. I do not think it is so and doubt that many other Christians think so, either. The question is, then, how can we be perceptive to the speaking of God?

Types of Dialogical Meditation

There are basically two approaches to the dialogical meditation: the imaginative and the passive receptive. The variations on these two modes of meditation are all but endless and so what I offer here should not be taken as limiting in any sense. Rather, these introductory comments should be taken as a springboard for further refinement.

In the tradition of Protestantism out of which I come the imagination is used very little. A great value is put on the use of words and upon rational discourse. Emotion is sometimes allowed, but always in its proper place and usually very carefully circumscribed by words. As I suggested above in chapter three, this essentially inhibits the development of the whole person, for the human being is also emotional, intuitive and nonrational. It has therefore been very exciting for me personally to discover the role that the imagination can play in making Christian experience meaningful. With some care the imagination can be called in to aid in the listening to the Divine leading in our everyday lives.

St. Teresa of Avila often used her imagination in meditating upon the faith. For her, as she described it, it was a way of experiencing the event as opposed to just reading about it in books. "Having gone through so much myself, I am sorry for those who begin with books alone, for it is extraordinary what a difference there is between understanding a thing and knowing it by experience."[3] The imaginative meditation opens up a variety of possibilities to experience which would normally be unavailable to a person. It might be that, during a time of decision about a course of action, God would speak to a person in the course of a meditation which is "running through" or "trying on for size" one or the other course of action, thereby revealing an insight of Divine origin in the decision process. There is no way of insuring that it will happen but if done honestly within the context of the expectation of God's speaking, it could happen. It still is appropriate to say, as in the case of the prophets of Israel, that God speaks to the person who listens.

The imaginative meditation can be a way of letting God speak to us by creating a format within which we can hear God. If one of the major reasons we do not hear God is because we do not listen, then it follows that if we were to design those conditions in which we could better listen, then we would be able to hear what God was saying to us. One reason we do not listen is because we are constantly distracted by the action and noise about us. It is exceedingly hard to pay attention to only one thing in this culture. Our minds are constantly chattering. The imaginative meditation allows us to enter into a meditative state of consciousness, thereby shutting out the distractions of a chattering mind and everything about us. It further centers down into the unconscious and allows God to utter that creative word which we often do not perceive. Creativity is one attribute of the Divine, and God speaks creatively in our soul, in our unconscious. It happens nightly in our dreams, I am convinced, and we don't pay much attention. In fact, we work very hard at forgetting what we dream and in general do not want to pay attention to the dreams we have. In any event, as our dreams are agents of revelation, so too can the imaginative meditation be.

The basic technique I use when I am wanting to be receptive to a contact with God in an imaginative mode of meditation is to construct a scene in which I can perceive God speaking to me. I might construct a scene in which I could have a conversation with a biblical character, possibly Jesus or Paul or one of the disciples. I might find it better to have a conversation with close friends I know and love, and who have often spoken the word of God to me in a given situation. It might be a scene in which a message could come in a different way. In general, I decide beforehand the mode and the general scene I will be trying, and then I give it a try. It is important to enter into the meditation with anticipation, and with reverence. We would do so with verbal prayer; we ought to do so also with imaginative prayer. This is not to say, however, that we do not on occasions enter into an imaginative meditation which might be joyous, or even just plain fun. In general, however one might enter into a time of verbal prayer is also a way in which one might enter into an imaginative encounter with the Divine.

It should also be emphasized that we must construct scenes in such a way that they are open-ended. We should try honestly not to "put words in God's mouth." This means we have to try not to presume in advance what the message or the answer to our question will be.

We are also to remember that we cannot force God into giving us an answer to a question. We sometimes forget that "no" is also an answer, and we often fail to allow God to say anything but "yes." We must also allow God to not answer. It may be that there is not an answer forthcoming. We should be prepared for that. We cannot presume to manipulate God into giving an answer. A certain humility is therefore to be desired in entering into the imaginative meditation of this sort.

The results from the imaginative dialogical meditation can be at once both surprising and beneficial. On one occasion this past spring, such a meditation occurred for me personally. The time was a particularly tense time in my life. The board of seminary administrators for which I was working was engaged in negotiations related to the future of our organization. It was a most unsettling time for our family because we could see that they were going to make a decision about the life or death of the institution, a decision which would obviously affect our future. We were not certain that we would be able to count on employment for very far into the future, and it seemed that at least we would have to leave our present home and move to another city to continue the work I was engaged in. It was a kind of situation in which many Americans must have found themselves over the past few years. Needless to say, we were distressed by the fact that our future was not in our hands and seemed to be in the hands of persons who had matters other than our future and well-being on their mind.

The situation, then, was one in which it was appropriate to ask, "Is there a word from the Lord?" I knew all kinds of answers and had no difficulty in theorizing all manner of responses which seemed to be appropriate Christian responses to the difficult time in which we found ourselves. The problem was that the answers seemed somewhat empty. They did not really capture my imagination. Although the answers were theologically sound, they were not truly internalized.

In the midst of this time, I remember specifically planning a dialogical meditation of an imaginative sort. In the meditative state I saw in my mind's eye that I was standing on the top of a sandy bluff overlooking the ocean. I was quite alone. The scene was very peaceful and gave me a feeling of being at home in the world.

The sun was warm, beating steadily on my shoulders and face. A gentle breeze came across the ocean, rustling my hair and clothing as it brought a fresh aroma of salty air. A few seagulls danced playfully across the deeply blue cloudless sky.

I started descending the bluff and started walking toward the ocean, all the time aware of the roar of the waves and the movement of the ocean as it reached out toward the beach and then withdrew in a gentle receding retreat. I turned and started walking along the beach. As I walked I looked out toward the horizon and noticed that there was a bottle floating on the water. As I stood watching, the bottle was tossed to and fro by the currents, now disappearing, now emerging again, but ever surely coming into the beach where I was waiting.

The feeling I had was one of anticipation. I knew that there was a message written for me in that bottle. I did not yet know what it was, since I had determined when planning the meditation that I would not decide in advance what the message was, only that there would probably be a message. I was excited when I waded out into the water to pick up the bottle and removed the cover to take out a slip of paper. With some trepidation I opened the paper and discovered there the words, "Hodie Christus natus est."

It was a surprising, indeed, a startling experience. The fact is, I don't often quote Latin to myself and the appearance of the message in Latin was totally unexpected. This often happens in meditation, if one truly does not program the answer in advance. This is one of the reasons I am convinced this kind of meditation is so valuable, because it allows our unconscious, and God through our inner being, to speak to us in a way we often do not expect.

The message itself was certainly appropriate. The phrase translates, "Today, Christ is born." What more did I really need in the time of distress in which I found myself? It was a message which affirmed the incarnational view I would no doubt articulate so willingly at other times, but this message bubbled up out of my depth and grabbed me by its suddenness and appropriateness. I had become so obsessed with the future that I had forgotten the central affirmation which gave meaning and hope for the present. When the words appeared to me on the page in the context of that meditation, it was not an idle affirmation of faith. Rather, it was a rekindling of faith down at the very roots of my being. In the midst of apparent insecurity, I discovered an insight into lasting security.

Waiting on the Lord

Another type of dialogical meditation which can be a very significant way of hearing what God wants to say to us is that kind of passive receptive meditation which waits for an image, insight, or thought to emerge from the depth of one's being. It is the kind of meditation which is known as "just sitting." Remember the story of the very old, very wise man who said, "Sometimes, I just sits and thinks, and sometimes I just sits." It is not an easy kind of meditation but it is potentially a powerful kind.

Although the various types of the dialogical prayer of waiting are related, perhaps it will be helpful to divide them for the purpose of better understanding. First, there is the most difficult prayer which seeks only to experience the Divine Presence. It is a presymbolic experiencing characterized by the immediacy of the awareness of the Presence. Words and images are not necessary.

As an act of Christian devotion it can be a most re-creating experience. As Kelly wrote, "deep within us all there is an amazing inner sanctuary of the soul, a holy place, a Divine Center, a speaking Voice, to which we may continuously return."[4] The prayer of quiet waiting seeks to turn to that Center and one may speak of the effort as "centering down." It is not an easy prayer to maintain without practice and the ability to experience it finally is a gift from God.

The prayer of quiet anticipation is called by various names. Often it is simply the prayer of silence, or contemplation, or perhaps more technically the *silentium mysticum*. It is the prayer which suggests that "beyond all thought and speech there lies a realm of exquisite silence."[5]

It is spoken of as "an intense and vivid silence: a silence which exists in itself, through and in spite of the ceaseless noises of your normal world."[6]

Thomas Merton speaks of the prayer of silence in his book, *Contemplative Prayer:*

> Contemplation is essentially a listening in silence, an expectancy. And yet in a certain sense, we must truly begin to hear God when we have ceased to listen. What is the explanation of this paradox? Perhaps only that there is a higher kind of listening, which is not an attentiveness to some special wave length, a receptivity to a certain kind of message, but a general emptiness that waits to realize the fullness of the message of God within its own apparent void. In other words, the true contemplative is not the one who prepared his mind for a particular message that he wants or expects to hear, but who remains empty because he knows that he can never expect or anticipate the word that will transform his darkness into light. He does not even an-

ticipate a special kind of transformation. He does not demand light instead of darkness. He waits on the Word of God in silence, and when he is "answered," it is not so much by a word that bursts into his silence. It is by his silence itself suddenly, inexplicably revealing itself to him as a word of great power, full of the voice of God.[7]

It is a difficult-to-reach but a nonetheless authentic dialogical form of meditation.

A second dialogical meditation of waiting is more easily described as "quiet observation." It is not a form in which meditation normally formulates specific questions to which answers are sought. Rather, it is a different way of seeing one's environment. As James Carroll says, "It is not that contemplation is the act of looking at the world and seeing something different. Contemplation is simply a different way of seeing."[8] In the meditative state a different context for the person is created. One becomes capable of seeing more than is simply before the eyes. It is more than seeing; it is perceiving.

A variety of alternatives can be appropriated in the method of quiet observation. A woman sitting in the garden might for the first time "see" her surroundings, truly perceiving the Presence in the natural surroundings about her. A man sitting in his den quietly watching his children at play might "see" them anew and perceive the Presence and become overwhelmingly aware of the gift which has been given to him.

In the time of quiet observation one's mind might leap to other thoughts, to other persons. The German theologican and martyr Dietrich Bonhoeffer incorporated what might appear to be wandering thoughts into a meditative practice: "Just sit down each day and wait patiently. If your thoughts keep running away, do not attempt to restrict them. It is no bother to let them run on to their destination; then, however, take up the place or the person to whom they have strayed into your prayers."[9]

Another form of the meditation of quiet observation is one which waits to see what images and feelings might emerge from the depths of one's own being. In a quiet, meditative state a person can sit very quietly and wait for the images which cross one's mind. I first learned this method from Bob Keck of the New Wineskins Center in Columbus. Bob suggested that it was possible to sit with pen in hand in a meditative state and record the images which emerge. I have found this to be a surprising way to enter into dialogue with myself and with God. Again, often we are so busy that we do not pay attention to the quiet ways in which God may be trying to get through to us. I would recommend keeping a journal of the images if anyone were interested in this approach. It would be over a longer period of time that the images would begin to have meaning. In general, I would suggest that the same methods be used for understanding the importance of the images that one uses in interpreting dreams.[10]

One might prefer to reach back behind the images which emerge and be receptive to feelings which might emerge. In the meditative state one could become aware of a feeling and then seek to find words and images which convey the meaning of that feeling. I think that God can well speak through feelings, and we often ignore this possibility as we ignore the feelings.

One place where the meditation of quiet observation seems particularly easy and appropriate is outdoors in the natural world. One might well even program some meditation of quiet observation in nature for the purpose of communing with God. Avery Brooke in a delightful book, *How to Meditate Without Leaving the World,* suggests some procedures for meditating on specific natural objects.[11] I have used his approach as a basis for group worship and found it not only liturgically but personally engaging. Elizabeth O'Conner in *Search for Silence* develops a usable exercise on "Contemplative Prayer and the Created Order"[12] which I can recommend for personal use.

One need not specifically program the meditation in nature, however. What is required simply is that one be prepared to engage in a bit of "seeing." Annie Dillard in her popular book, *Pilgrim at Tinker Creek,* describes an experience which is both an example of quiet observation and a description of the possible kinds of benefits which accrue to the one who practices it. She describes her search for a wonderful tree which she calls the "tree with the lights in it":

> It was for this tree I searched through the peach orchards of summer, in the forests of fall and down winter and spring for years. Then one day I was walking along Tinker Creek thinking of nothing at all and I saw the tree with the lights in it. I saw the backyard cedar where the mourning doves roost charged and transfigured, each cell buzzing with flame. I stood on the grass with the lights in it, grass that was wholly fire, utterly focused and utterly dreamed. It was less like seeing than like being for the first time seen, knocked breathless by a powerful glance. The flood of fire abated, but I'm still spending the power. Gradually the lights went out in the cedar, the colors died, the cells unflamed and disappeared. I was still ringing. I had been my whole life a bell, and never knew it until at that moment I was lifted and struck.[13]

The Occasions for Dialogical Meditation

What are the variety of occasions in which one might wish to make use of dialogical meditation? This is another way of asking the question, what are the varied purposes of dialogical meditation? The following suggestions will not be exhaustive, but perhaps they will provide a stimulus to further ideas.

1. *Preparation.* One might wish to use this form of meditation prior to beginning the day. One member of our meditation group will begin every day by visualizing in a meditative state what she has to be involved in during that particular day. It is more than a case of mentally rehearsing what she is about to do prior to the task. It is a part of her enlisting her own capacities and the help of God in what she will be doing. Not only will she be better able to do what she intends or needs to do, she will often receive valuable insights into the motivation for certain tasks, the way she should accomplish them,

and the relative priority of various tasks. A variation on this approach is to use the imaginative meditation prior to any particular task. We often pray before a task and we would not pray to be able to do what we are incapable of, but only to do what we can as well as possible. The dialogical meditation is one means of praying for such divine guidance.

2. *Decision Making.* One might use the dialogical meditation in the midst of an impending decision. One might ask oneself what it is that one wants to do and then wait to see what images and insights arise to provide input for the making of the decision. Another approach, and a very interesting one, might be to consider the alternatives of a decision by visualizing the alternatives in the meditation. That is, if there were two courses of action open which required a decision, the meditator could pursue each of those alternatives in the course of the imaginative meditation in order to see how comfortable he or she felt in the experience, to see what the implications of the actions might be. A third approach might be to enter into a discussion within the context of an imaginative meditation with a trusted friend and confidant to gain some perspective on the decision.

3. *Self-knowledge.* The dialogical meditation is particularly helpful in providing insights to a person as to who he or she really is. One of the important tasks we can perform in the dialogical meditation is to seek to know ourselves better. Self-knowledge has often been neglected in the church, and yet it is one of the most important goals of the Christian. So much that is destructive in Christian behavior results from an absence of self-knowledge. This has been long recognized in the church. John Calvin began his magnum opus, the *Institutes,* with just that recognition: "Nearly all the wisdom we possess, that is to say, true and sound wisdom, consists of two parts: the knowledge of God and of ourselves." [14] Through meditation we can be open to both kinds of knowledge.

4. *Knowledge of God.* Often the knowledge of the self leads to the knowledge of God. As we find ourselves to be sinners, we come to recognize the need for the Redeemer, for example. God is, of course, to be found many ways. One certain benefit of the dialogical meditation is to discover the message of God for the particular moment in which one is engaged. The variety of ways one might go about this are many, but one should enlist the imagination in finding ways to be open to the knowledge of God.

5. *Understanding Others.* The dialogical meditation can give us the means whereby we can understand other persons. We are often so quick to criticize another person, and the fact is, we usually do it for the wrong reason. We seldom understand exactly why people do what they do, make the choices they make, and act how they act. Understanding human motivation is a tricky matter, but it would be helpful if on occasion we could "walk in another's shoes." The dialogical meditation can allow us to do that, and perhaps we'll derive a perspective therefrom which will help in our relations to others. We also might use the dialogical meditation to understand our relations to others. Perhaps we experience conflict with another person. Either by imaginatively "putting on" the other person in a conversation with us or by observing a conversation between us, we might just learn why the conflict exists. Even if we are thereby not able to resolve the conflict, we might at least be more accepting of the other and ourselves in the relationship. Then unrealistic expectations could well be revised.

Judging the Validity of Insights

One of the great dangers in using dialogical meditations is the temptation to accept uncritically the revelations which come as divine commands to perform certain actions. I think it would be fair to say that the revelations we receive are valid, but they may be only revelations of how our own internal state is ambivalent about any particular course of action. Recognizing that ambivalence is potentially very helpful, but to choose one path over another simply because it came in a meditation would be a dangerous route to go. In the first place, to use meditations for this purpose is effectively to avoid taking the responsibility for decisions. If we can point to our revelation as the reason for our action, then we don't have to take the responsibility for our choices. I don't believe that God would really want us to function that way. Therefore, even when we have received certain insights in the course of our meditation, we still have to have some standards by which we judge the advisability of the particular choices which are to be made, and we have to be willing ultimately to take the responsibility for our actions. In addition, we should not automatically assume that the insights which we glean from the meditation are necessarily consistent with the Divine Will. We must still be able to discern the insights by certain standards.

The necessity of judging whether a word from God is indeed from God and is not a false revelation is a problem of ancient origins. The ancient Hebrews also wrestled with the question. In the midst of often conflicting prophetic assertions expressed as coming from Yahweh, the writer of Deuteronomy provided some help: "If you ask yourselves, 'How shall we recognize a word that the Lord has not uttered?' this is the answer: When the word spoken by the prophet in the name of the LORD is not fulfilled and does not come true, it is not a word spoken by the LORD. The prophet has spoken presumptuously; do not hold him in awe." (Deut. 18:21-22) One simple test for the Deuteronomist was, if what was offered as a revelation from God did not work out as it was predicted, if it did not in fact correspond to truth and reality, then it was a false word.

This is an interesting passage because it suggests that even the Hebrews had problems with trying to discern what was the authentic message from Yahweh, and it suggests that one approach to discerning the truth of a message was to measure it against perceived reality. If it didn't wash, it wasn't from Yahweh.

A "wait and see" attitude might be acceptable for certain matters but it would be dangerous in others. Was there not any way to discern whether a revelation was indeed from Yahweh before one acted on it? In Deuteronomy thirteen the writer says, "When a prophet or dreamer appears among you and offers you a sign or a portent and calls on you to follow other gods whom you have not known and worship them, even if the sign or portent should come true, do not listen to the words of that prophet or that dreamer. God is testing you through him to discover whether you love the LORD your God with all your heart and soul. You must follow the LORD your God and fear him; you must keep his commandments and obey him, serve him and hold fast to him." (Deut. 13:1-4)

There is indeed a way to judge the revelations which are offered, and it is not merely a trial and error approach. The writer of Deuteronomy is saying that the test is whether or not the dreamer or prophet, or in our case the meditator, calls the person back to the earlier revelations from God and calls the person to commitment to God with all of the being, "with all your heart and soul." One tests our later utterances by the earlier action of God in history.

This means that we too must have a certain and firm understanding of where we stand in the faith *before* we begin to look for the Word from God in our own experiences. We will then need to be aware of what the principles are by which we do in fact judge the truth or falsity of any claim on our allegiance.

This is not the place to set forth definitively what I think those standards or canons might be, but it is important to say at least that as Christians we must first determine what our understanding of the principles are. For Christians the starting point is Christological. The Lordship of Christ is the beginning standard by which one judges. As Paul said, "No one can say 'Jesus is Lord!' except under the influence of the Holy Spirit." (I Cor. 12:3)

There are other further affirmations which form the basis of making the judgments. For me the judgments often turn on the basis of whether the graciousness of God is revealed or whether in some sense I am refusing to let God save me by grace and not by works. At other times the judgment might be made on the basis of understanding God as a Liberating God who calls for love, or perhaps the Creating God who calls for a caring response to all of creation.

What I am saying is that the individual Christian will have to have some awareness by which to judge whether or not the particular insights which have come through meditation have come from God. It is not as difficult as it sounds, but it is as important as it can be. We do not and cannot abdicate our responsibility for our own lives and actions.

Interlude: How to Use the Meditations in This Book

The imaginative meditations which are included in this book are designed to be samples of the kind of meditation a person or a group might use.

It is not imperative for the use of these meditations to be restricted to groups, but it is thought that such will be the most common use. Suggestions are given in chapter nine on the place of Christian meditation in the local church. It would be well to read that chapter before proceeding to the practice of the following meditations.

The meditations which follow set forth the purpose and procedure of the individual meditations before giving the meditation itself. Suggestions follow the meditation for debriefing.

As to the meditations themselves, the guide should feel free to alter the text in any appropriate fashion. The meditations are printed here as they would be spoken in a group. The guide can either read the meditation as is, record it on tape, say it from memory, or use notes. The point is, the meditations can be used as is, or they can be altered as necessary.

The meditation should be said slowly and deliberately, giving adequate opportunities between sentences for the group to experience the scene. Certain key phrases referring to visual and sensory phenomena are included in the meditations which are designed to enhance the experience. These types of phrases should be included in any meditation used in a group. If the meditator is able to experience movement, a variety of sights and sounds, and even the sense of touch during a meditation, then the likelihood of a more successful meditation is created.

An individual may use these meditations also. This may be accomplished by either recording the meditation and listening to the tape or by reading the meditation beforehand and then experiencing the meditation afterwards in a meditative state of consciousness.

The first meditation gives a relaxation exercise. It is essential for the induction of the meditative state. The exercise included here can be used in the initial stages of the group. Variations are encouraged. As the group progresses it will need less extensive relaxation exercises. Other relaxation procedures may be found in *Passages*[15] and in the *Centering Book*.[16]

Meditation: The Friends in the Meadow

PURPOSE

By means of an imaginary encounter with friends in a meadow, conversations are held which will allow matters of concern to you at this moment in time to emerge from your inner being. The basic goal of this meditation is to gain self-knowledge and possible insights which might emerge. Therefore, the general framework is programmed, but the basic insights which might emerge are left open. A variation of this meditation might be to work with a particular problem or concern in mind.

PROCEDURE

Prior to beginning the meditation, allow the meditators or yourself to find a comfortable position. Some will want to lie down. Others will want to sit straight in a chair. Perhaps some will want to remove their shoes. You might wish to lower the lights and to make sure that there will be no interruptions during the course of the meditation.

I personally prefer briefly to outline for the group the meditation which is to take place. I will expand on the reasons for this in Chapter nine, but basically it is so there will be no surprises to distract the meditators and so the meditators will be better able to trust my direction during the course of the meditation. You might say something like the following:

"I am going to lead you in a relaxation exercise. Afterwards we will start out on a hill overlooking some woods. We will descend a path into the woods, coming out into a meadow where we will have the opportunity to talk with some friends briefly before coming out on the other side. Do not decide yet who you will see or what the nature of the conversations will be. Let your inner being decide that for you in the meditation."

THE RELAXATION EXERCISE

Now by the intent of your mind you are going to become deeply, deeply relaxed. You will enter into a journey with yourself which will be pleasurable and comfortable, but to facilitate your journey better you will need to be very relaxed.

We are going to take a few moments to become more deeply relaxed. You will be aware of my voice and perhaps of other sounds about you, but you will be paying attention to my voice and will be aware of the inner journey you are making. You will be awake and alert for the trip but very gently relaxed.

You might want to begin by taking a few deep breaths, letting each breath symbolize for you that you are becoming relaxed. As you breathe in, imagine that you are breathing in peace and relaxation; as you breathe out, let the tension and anxiety flow out of your body. You are becoming very deeply, deeply relaxed.

Now direct the attention of your mind's eye to the muscles in your feet and ankles. Imagine that the muscles there are becoming very loose and relaxed. Imagine what it must be like for the muscles to become relaxed. Perhaps with the breathing in and out of the air you can let the tension and tightness flow out of your body.

(Pause five seconds)

Now let your attention focus on the muscles of the calves of your legs and imagine that they are becoming very deeply relaxed.

(Pause five seconds)

Address your attention now to the muscles in the thighs of your legs. Let the muscles there become very deeply relaxed. Just let go and let the muscles of your legs become completely relaxed—breathing in peace and relaxation, breathing out tension and anxiety.

(Pause five seconds)

Now address your attention to the muscles in your hips. Let the muscles become very relaxed. After your hip muscles have let go and relaxed, let your attention shift to the muscles in your solar plexus, to the muscles in your abdomen and in your lower back. Let the muscles just become very deeply, deeply relaxed—breathing in peace and relaxation; breathing out tension, tightness and anxiety.

Let your mind's eye now wander to your chest muscles and the muscles in your upper back, once again letting those muscles become very relaxed. With each breath you are becoming very deeply relaxed.

Now take just a moment to image that the muscles are relaxing in your shoulders and arms, beginning with the upper arms and descending down to each finger in your hand. You are becoming very relaxed.

(Pause five seconds)

Look in your mind's eye now to the muscles in your neck and in the back of your head. Let the muscles there become very relaxed. Let your attention move over your scalp and to your face and let the muscles become very deeply relaxed. Here is a place we often hold in tension without being aware of it. Be sure to let the muscles around your eyes and in your forehead become very relaxed.

Now you are deeply relaxed, more deeply relaxed than you have been at any time today. Take just a moment to survey the muscles of your body, and if you note any place where there is tightness, just let that tightness flow out of your body with your very next breath.

(Pause five seconds)

THE MEDITATION

Now that you are deeply relaxed we are going to take a short journey into your inner being. You are awake and alert to the sound of my voice and the trip we are taking, even though you are deeply relaxed.

In your mind's eye visualize that you are standing on the peak of a grassy hill somewhere. Be aware that you are standing alone, looking off into the distance where lying before you at the end of a short path is a clump of woods. It is a comfortable day. The sun is shining. Birds are singing. A gentle breeze is blowing. Be aware that the breeze is blowing slowly through the grass about you. There are flowers growing here and there around you. Notice the colors and perhaps become aware of the fragrance about you.

Begin, now, to descend at a comfortable pace the path lying before you. Be aware of your feet stepping on the path. Note how it feels as you continue your descent towards the woods.

Now you are entering into the woods and are continuing along the path. Notice that it is perceptibly cooler as you continue walking. Be aware of the variety of trees, of bushes, of flowers blossoming about you as you continue walking deeper and deeper into the woods. Look out to the side and notice that here and there the sun breaks through the trees and starts shadows dancing about the woods as the wind rustles through the leaves. You are glad to be here. It is a comfortable feeling tempered by a sense of anticipation as you move deeper into the woods, but coming now to the end of the woods as the path leads out into a meadow.

As you reach the end of the path in the woods, stop for a second and look out across the meadow. There the sun shines uninhibited on the grass and flowers. Notice that a small brook runs through the meadow, dividing the area. About halfway across the meadow is a small bridge which connects the two parts of the pasture.

As you stand here at the meadow's edge and look out into the near distance, become aware that there are a few people standing and milling about not far away, just this side of the bridge. As you begin making your way toward the people, you become aware that these are friends of yours. Perhaps you have not seen some of these friends for a long time, and perhaps they are people you have just recently been with.

As you come closer to them you are going to have the opportunity to visit briefly with a few of them, in whatever fashion is appropriate, perhaps by conversing, or perhaps by just sensing each other's presence. Whatever the mode of conversation, you do not need to stop now and think about the meaning of the conversation or why you are talking about the particular subjects that emerge. Just enjoy the presence of your friends and move from friend to friend at a comfortable pace. You will have a few minutes to experience the conversations.

(Pause four minutes)

Now it is time for you to continue on your way. Start saying good-bye to your friends, and start making your way on through them toward the bridge. As you start across the bridge, hear someone call your name. Stop and turn back a few steps, and see that one of your friends is coming toward you. This friend has a gift to give you. Accept the gift gratefully. Thank your friend and continue on your way, carrying your gift. Do not think about the conversations or the significance of the particualr gift. As you cross the bridge, you come now to an exit from the pasture where you once again take up a path and enter into the woods.

Continue along the path a short ways, stepping upward on the gently sloping incline, coming now to the end of the woods on the other side from whence you began your journey.

As you continue up the path now, begin to come back to the level of consciousness in which you normally are living. Come back at your own pace, perhaps beginning to do in reverse the relaxation exercise. As you begin to come back to awareness, you can begin to stretch your muscles so that you finally come back to full normal consciousness.

Welcome back.

DEBRIEFING

With this kind of meditation you can never be sure which direction you will go. It certainly is nothing you can force. I usually wait to see if anything in particular emerges from the group. Since this will be done in all likelihood in a small group, there should be opportunity to discuss what happened if the participants so choose.

There are questions which you might ask to stimulate the discussion, such as, did you learn anything you did not already know? Did anything surprising happen? What happened that you would like to share? Were the friends the ones you expected or others? Who gave you the gift? What was the significance of this person bringing a gift to you? What was the gift? Is there any connection you can think of between that gift and the person? Did you learn anything new about yourself in this meditation?

Meditation: A Walk Through the Park

PURPOSE

To provide a creative medium for your inner being to communicate to you something you may be ignoring in normal consciousness. This meditation may also be tried out as a variation of problem-solving dialogical meditation. Simply indicate to yourself before entering into the meditation that this will be an attempt to provide insight into the particular problem you have in mind. Say to yourself, "I am seeking an answer to . . ." or "I would like an insight into . . ." Although you cannot force the answer to come forth, it may be that you will gain insights you can use.

PROCEDURE

Ask your group to find their way into comfortable positions as indicated in the previous meditation. Indicate something of the nature of this meditation and what your goals might be. Indicate what kind of a relaxation exercise you will try. After your group has some facility, it will not be necessary to prolong the relaxation, and you can try variations. In fact, after the group has been engaged in meditation for some time, it will possibly only take a few breaths and the expressed intention of the mind to bring about the state of relaxation.

Say something like the following prior to the meditation: This meditation will consist of a walk through a busy park scene. You will walk through the park, coming to a choice of paths, which choice you will make. The path you take will eventually lead you out of the park to the front of the park where you will see a person drawing a scene on the sidewalk with chalk. You will then look at the scene before leaving the part altogether and ending the meditation.

THE MEDITATION

Now in your mind's eye imagine that you standing in the midst of a large park which extends for acres in every direction.

It is a sunny day, and the temperature is mild. You are on vacation, perhaps, and you are taking the time to stroll along comfortably. Nothing particular is on your mind. Enjoy the stroll as you walk across a large grassy field.

Look off into the distance and note that in one direction you can see a ball game of some sort underway. In the other direction is a pond on which there are possibly some ducks swimming about.

As you walk along, you will come to a path which seems to divide the park, cutting right through the middle of the recreational areas. Continue walking along this path, paying attention to the many different sights and sounds that come your way. It is a lazy sort of day, one which you are thoroughly enjoying.

You come now to a division of paths. You have not been this way before, and it seems to be a less travelled section of the park just at this time. Stand for a moment and decide which path you will take, knowing that you can explore only one at the moment and that this will mean that there are experiences along one path that you will not be able to enjoy at this time. Choose your path now and continue along it.

The path you have chosen continues a short way around a clump of trees and bushes. It brings you, as you walk, to a wrought-iron fence which appears to surround the park. You are, in fact, walking along the park fence and are coming to the entrance to the park. Continue along the path and out of the entrance and note that you are standing on a broad expanse of sidewalk.

Take just a moment to look around and see what it is that is around you. Look across the sidewalk and across the street. Note what the buildings are which face the park.

As you look down the sidewalk, notice that there is a sidewalk artist working on a drawing not far from you now. Walk over to the place where the artist is working and look at the painting. Take a few moments now to stand and look at the painting which is being constructed before you. Be aware of the colors and of the scene which is being made. Do not now try to make any particular sense out of the meaning of the picture. Just look at it. Be aware of the feelings which you have as you look at it, and now for a couple of minutes just enjoy it.

(Pause two minutes)

Now it is time for you to continue along your way. Knowing that you can return here anytime you wish, begin making your way along the sidewalk, away from the park and away from the sidewalk artist. Come back to the normal state of consciousness at your own pace.

DEBRIEFING

Again, allow the conversation to go however your group seems to take it. You might then ask some leading questions, such as, What kind of a park was it? How did you feel? Did you notice anything unusual? How did you feel about the choice of the paths? Did you have any difficulty making a choice? How did you feel about the path you did not take? What do you think was there? Are you glad you took the path you did? What was the scene across from the park? Was the artist a man or a woman? Was it anyone you knew? What was the picture? What do you think was the significance or meaning for you of the picture?

6
Story Meditation: Exploring the Bible as a Participant

Once upon a time . . . Say, let me tell you a story . . . Hey, do you know a good story?

These familiar lines all point to the easily recognizable fact that our lives are constantly in touch with stories. We are either telling one or listening to one much of the time. What would life be like without stories?

Before bed at night my children want to hear a story. Usually it's one they pick out from their bookshelves, but sometimes my seven-year-old Nancy will say, "Tell me a story about when you were a little boy." Who can resist the opportunity to tell, or hear, a story?

One of the encouraging developments in theological circles in recent years is the awakening of interest in "story" and its relation to thinking thoughts about God and humanity. Articles have started appearing in scholarly journals on "The Narrative Quality of Experience" and "Parable, Metaphor and Theology."[1] Serious scholars publish books with such titles as *Religion as Story, Biography as Theology* and *Fantasy and the Human Spirit.*[2] One of America's leading theologians contributes an invitation to religious studies which leans heavily on story, and he calls his work by the imaginative title, *Ascent of the Mountain, Flight of the Dove.*[3]

The Importance of Story

Why is there this rekindling of interest in stories? Why do we love stories so much would perhaps be a better question. What is it about a story that so easily attracts our attention and our imagination?

There seems to be an intimate connection between life itself and the telling of a story, as if the story were a way of taking hold of life and making sense of it. Ted Estess puts it succintly: "As Samuel Becket writes, 'To have lived is not enough. . . . [We] have to talk about it.' And one important way of talking about life is to shape its vagaries into the form of a story."[4]

It's true that stories are entertaining, but there is more to our attachment to stories than mere recreation. Stories are more re-creation than recreation. As we give ourselves to a story, we enlarge our capacity for experiencing life. We live beyond ourselves in stories and in doing so increase the options of our daily living. As Sallie TeSelle says, "We love stories . . . because our lives are stories and we recognize in the attempts of others to move, temporally and painfully, our own story."[5]

Stories give order to our lives and to existence. As children hear story after story, they are becoming initiated into the human society around them. There is a sense in which the story functions to make us human. Perhaps the capacity for story is what distinguishes us as human beings and not mere animals.

Living Our Story

We live our lives as a story. We too have a beginning, a middle and an end. We also have a story line or a plot which we are living out. We make sense out of our lives by choosing a particular story to live.

A particular time period in my life, in my own story, reminds me of the power of story. I was working in a coffeehouse run by Center Church in Hartford, Connecticut. It was in the mid-sixties, a time of great youth disaffection in our country. The drug subculture had been growing, and untold numbers of teen-aged youth were acting out their frustrations with the dominant middle-class culture by "dropping out." The coffeehouse movement was in part a response to the youth crisis, and Christian coffeehouses sprang up all over the country and served as places where kids could come and "be themselves."

This particular coffeehouse in Hartford had a clientele characterized by two completely different story lines. It was a fascinating scene to watch, for we had two clearly definable groups composed of youths of the same approximate age, who had come out of different socioeconomic and educational backgrounds. They had consequently chosen two completely different stories to live out their lives.

The first group to come saw themselves as "flower children" or hippies. They were by and large the children of middle-class, successful parents. It's easy to remember how they looked: long hair, a few beards on those old enough to shave, blue jeans, beads, and bare feet. These kids had generally adopted for themselves the story they saw being played out on television and in the news magazines. Perhaps in some ways they were the creation of the news media. They were a gentle group who loved poetry and listened to the music of the Beatles and Bob Dylan. And they were into drugs. The sacraments of this culture bore strange names like pot and hash and acid. The story these kids had chosen for themselves was a fairly consistent one. There were few deviations.

The second group, composed of young men approximately the same age, had also chosen a story that took them outside the normal conventions of society. They were a motorcycle gang. Their uniform was consistent: dirty blue jeans, sleeveless denim jacket, boots, and black leather jacket. They were not gentle in appearance or action. They preferred beer to drugs and clearly despised the hippies. After several months of standing between the bikers and the hippies, it became clear that I was watching the unfolding of a type-B movie before my eyes. These kids had modeled themselves after their heroes and were living out their stories, choosing even the vocabulary and style of interacting for which their particular stories called.

There was very little deviation from the chosen story lines. Whether the stories had been consciously chosen, I could not say, but it was clear that once the story had been chosen, a particular set of options were open to the individuals in the respective groups, and a particular set of options were closed. In fact, decisions were all but preordained by the chosen story. It was a clear case of life imitating art.

Story and Christian Faith

If the story we choose to live out does, in fact, determine how our choices will be made and thereby will determine our future as we attempt to give meaning to our lives, then it becomes very important for the Christian to become aware of this in choosing an appropriate story.

Christianity is essentially a story. It is a story about the activity of God in history, especially in the person of Jesus the Christ, but also in his followers who have chosen to live out a particular story.

As we hear our sacred stories, we find that our lives are shaped by them. We do not make up the stories which we decide will become sacred for us. Instead, the stories themselves speak to us, and we awaken to them. Consciousness itself " . . . is molded by the sacred story to which it awakens."[6]

It is a particular chosen story which is to be the dominant factor in our living our lives. We often refer to an individual as a person of principle, but it is the story more than the principle which determines how he or she will act. As Michael Novak says:

A person does not live primarily by principles but by stories. And he or she comes to each situation as if it were a new episode in a story. One's personal story carries with it one's internalized experience, reflection, and sensitivity developed over the years. One comes to a situation, not newborn, but already in mid-course. One's tone of voice, mannerisms, intuitions and sensitivities reveal the "role" one is implicitly playing out.[7]

We would do well to choose our stories with care.

Not only do we choose certain stories to live as our own, we are very actively involved in telling stories. Our faith is given shape and form and substance as we tell our stories. Christianity itself spread throughout the Mediterranean world by the telling of a story. It was a particularly Jewish way of communicating, as it still is. How often a Jewish rabbi will make his point by telling a story. In fact a Jewish philosopher will do the same. A Jewish story will illustrate the power of story:

When the Baal Shem had a difficult task before him, he would go to a certain place in the woods, light a fire and meditate in prayer—and what he had set out to perform was done. When a generation later the "Maggid" of Meseritz was faced with the same task he would go to the same place in the woods and say: We can no longer light the fire, but we can still speak the prayers—and what he wanted done became reality. Again a generation later Rabbi Moshe Leib Sassov had to perform this task. And he too went into the woods and said: We can no longer light a fire, nor do we know the secret meditations belonging to the prayer, but we do know the place in the woods to which it all belongs—and that must be sufficient; and sufficient it was. But when another generation had passed and Rabbi Israel of Rishin was called upon to perform the task, he sat down on his golden chair in his castle and said: We cannot light the fire, we cannot speak the prayers, we do not know the place, but we can tell the story of how it was done. And . . . the story which he told had the same effect as the actions of the other three.[8]

Why does the telling of a story have such power? It is not simply because it is a good way of making a point in an argument or in a speech. Nor does the power of a story merely lie in the fact that it allows you to illustrate a desired conclusion so that an audience will understand what it is you are trying to say. The power of story lies much deeper. It lies in the nature of the medium of story itself and in the response it calls forth from the human being.

In the early sixties a brilliant and original critic, Marshall McLuhan, burst upon the intellectual scene with a controversial book, *Understanding Media: The Extensions of Man.* In this work McLuhan raises some significant questions about the modern world and the effect which communications has on the development of humanity. One of the basic insights which McLuhan makes in his book is helpful for understanding the power of story.

McLuhan defined media as being either hot or cool:

> There is a basic principle that distinguishes a hot medium like radio from a cool one like the telephone, or a hot medium like the movie from a cool one like TV. A hot medium is one that extends one single sense in "high definition." High definition is the state of being well filled with data. A photograph is, visually, "high definition." A cartoon is "low definition," simply because very little visual information is provided. Telephone is a cool medium or one of low definition, because the ear is given a meager amount of information. And speech is a cool medium of low definition, because so little is given and so much has to be filled in by the listener. On the other hand, hot media do not leave so much to be filled in or completed by the audience. Hot media are, therefore, low in participation, and cool media are high in participation or completion by the audience.[9]

A "hot medium" is one that does everything for you. It requires no participation on your part; it does not involve you. A "cool medium" is one that requires that you participate in it in some way in order to make sense out of it or to enjoy it. A cool medium therefore involves you and, in a sense, forces you to turn on your inner mind in order to participate.

One of the best examples of a cool medium is the TV commercial. In just one minute a message has to get across to the audience, and there is not time to fill in all the background which brought the watcher to this particular time. So we watch a commercial with a couple carrying in some bags from their station wagon, and we "fill in the blanks." They must have gone shopping, and now they are home carrying in the groceries. A child or a neighbor has seen them arrive and has come over. A conversation starts. This kind of commercial vignette requires that we be actively involved in filling in the background in order to make sense out of the commercial. It is a cool medium because it necessitates our participation, and once we participate in it, we become a part of it.

Story is a cool medium. We have to fill in the background in at least one crucial way: our imagination pictures the scene about which we are hearing or reading. The best and most engaging kind of story is one in which we become involved. Why are the writings of Agathie Christie so popular? It's not because they are great literature, but because she discovered a way to involve her readers. She distributes clues throughout her mysteries, and the alert person can pick them up and "solve" the crime even before Hercule Poirot or Miss Marple. It is a cool medium because it involves the reader's imagination.

Story does what mere arguments or propositions or lists of points of view cannot do. Such arguments or propositions only enlist the left-brain, but a story enlists the left and the right-brain. This means that the story begins to involve the whole person, as our rational and imaginative sides enter into the story. As Carroll says, "The great thing about the story we tell is this: in telling we become part of it. The time and place of the story includes not only Jerusalem all those years ago, but here and now, and there and tomorrow."[10]

This is the reason why the Bible is so powerful in the impact it makes. We do not read long lists of doctrines or assertions about God. We read stories. We do not find an assertion, "God is Creator." Rather we read these marvelous stories in Genesis. We do not read that "God is sovereign and man is not." Instead, we read that story about Job. We do not read an argument developing the assertion that "God is a loving God." What we do read are stories about a man named Jesus who represents in his very life and death the truth that God is love.

There is more to the Bible than just stories, of course. But the stories are there, and they may be the most important part for us. What we want to be able to do is to experience what we read about in the Bible, and we can do this when we tell the story. We can then make the story line our story line. The plot becomes our plot. We become the actors as we live the story.

It is at this point that meditation can help us. Meditation allows us to experience the biblical story ourselves through the story meditation. As we experience a story meditation, we are using both the left and the right brain, and we experience the story as a whole person. It is as we experience the stories ourselves and begin to live the stories as our stories that the "faith of our fathers" becomes a living faith as it becomes our faith.

Let me illustrate this point by telling a story, the story of Moses recorded in the early chapters of Exodus.

The Story of Moses

The story of Moses begins with the move of the Children of Israel to Egypt during the great famine. After the death of Joseph, a new king came to the throne in Egypt. This king was threatened by the presence of the Israelites in Egypt. He took severe measures to subject them to his control, consigning them to oppressive labor battalions and finally decreeing that all of the males born to the Israelites were to be murdered. When Moses was born, however, he was not killed. Instead, he was put into a small basket and put into the river so that he sailed into the midst of the company of the Pharoah's daughter while they were bathing.

Moses' sister had followed along with the basket so that when the Pharoah's daughter took him out of the water and recognized that he was a Hebrew child, Miriam was there to offer a Hebrew woman—Moses' mother—as a wet nurse. Hence, Moses had the double opportunity of growing up in the house of Pharoah, thereby learning the advantages of power and leadership, and in his own house, thereby learning what it meant to be a Hebrew.

Finally the identification with the Hebrews on Moses' part forced him to make a choice that led to his fleeing the country. Moses killed an Egyptian who was striking one of the Hebrews. After he recognized that his cover was blown, Moses left Egypt and found himself next in Midian, where he married the daughter of the Midianite priest, Jethro. Apparently his father-in-law took him on as a helper, and Moses next found himself minding the flocks of his father-in-law and, in fact, he was wandering around in the Sinai desert with the sheep. At that point Moses had an experience that was to change his life, and the course of history. He met the God of Abraham, Isaac, and Jacob in the Burning Bush and received the commission which led to his return to Egypt to lead the Israelites out of oppression. The Exodus came to be the central redemptive event in the formation of the Nation Israel.

The bare bones of the story of Moses as recounted above from the first three chapters of Exodus is a remarkable story. What strikes me in the story of Moses at this particular point, however, is not the drama of it, although it is certainly there, even as briefly outlined above. What really strikes my imagination is the suspicion that story had a lot to do with Moses' appearance.

When Moses was brought up by his mother, he was clearly brought up as a Hebrew. She did Moses and all of Israel a service by doing that. The question comes to mind, however, as to what she must have done to make Moses the sensitive person he was. I think Moses' mother did for Moses what any mother does for her children: she told him stories, stories about the exploits of a nomadic people led by such giants as Abraham, Isaac and Jacob. It is not hard for me to imagine, and I think it in no way does an injustice to the text, that Moses was brought up with a particularly intense dose of stories about the fathers in the faith. It was this that led him so quickly to identify with the Hebrew who was being oppressed by the Egyptian and to take the action he took. What is remarkable in that story is not that Moses killed the Egyptian but that Moses identified with the Hebrew, and he did this because of the stories he had heard as a child on his mother's knee. It was story which gave Moses his identity, so that he became identified with the oppressed and the disenfranchised. This in itself is remarkable, but there is more.

As Moses was tending the flock of his father-in-law, I think story came to play an even more important role in his life. I can well imagine that it does not take much conscious effort to tend sheep. I don't know this for sure, but I suspect that, once you really learn the art, it becomes a kind of second nature for you to react sufficiently to take care of the sheep. This would seem to free the mind to wander, a state almost like the meditative state on occasion.

My own imagination has constructed what I think happened, but, again, I don't believe that it does the text an injustice. What must have happened is that Moses was keeping the sheep of Jethro and was at the same time reflecting upon what it was that had brought him to this place. Moses had become a Midianite, in effect, but he could not forget his past, and as he wandered around in the wilderness with time on his hands, he was living the life of his fathers. He had become a nomad himself, and I rather expect that the stories his mother had told him about Abraham, Isaac and Jacob came alive to him in the dim shadows of the Sinai desert. Did Moses recall these words: "The LORD said to Abram, 'Leave your own country, your kinsmen, and your father's house, and go to a country that I will show you. I will make you into a great nation, I will bless you and make your name so great that it shall be used in blessings.' " (Gen. 12:1–2) If not these words, then words like them, and it must have been that there in the Sinai desert Moses began self-consciously to relive the story of his Hebrew forefathers. As he began to relive that story as his own story, God came to him in the Burning Bush.

In the same way, then, for us we can begin to live the story lines of the biblical stories as our own stories, and as we do so, our own identities will be shaped and formed, and we too will become the people of God. The biblical stories are not just stories about what happened. They are stories about what happens. This is the reason that the Bible is so powerful, because the stories are our stories.

The story meditation as a biblical meditation is a powerful way for us to relive the stories of the Bible as our stories and to find out by our participation in the stories themselves what the implications of those stories are for our own lives.

Meditation: A Visit with the Apostle Paul

PURPOSE

The purpose of this meditation is to have a conversation with the Apostle Paul on the nature of love and its meaning for Christians.

BACKGROUND

The church at Corinth was one of the favorites of the Apostle Paul. Located in a populous Greek city Paul spent more time there than in any of the churches he founded, except for Ephesus. Corinth itself was known for its debauchery, and if you wanted to accuse one of such, you would say that he or she lived "like a Corinthian." Paul was probably in Corinth beginning in the winter or spring of A.D. 50 and stayed for eighteen months.

Some years later word came to Paul there were problems at Corinth, and the letter to the Corinthians reveals that there was a distressing sort of moral laxity. There were divisions in the church, reaching even to the point of the formation of different cliques. There was sexual immorality. Christians were fighting against Christians even in the pagan law courts, certainly a disgraceful spectacle to Paul. There were disorders in the worship services at Corinth, evidenced even with abuses in the practice of the Lord's Supper. And there were apparent disagreements over spiritual gifts, with some saying that the highest gift certainly must have been that of speaking in tongues, while others said that it was prophecy.

If one keeps in mind how much Paul must have loved the Corinthians, it becomes clear that he must have been very discouraged as he was writing the letter. It is in the midst of the discussions on spiritual gifts that Paul offers one of the highest points of his writings, the Hymn to Love of 1 Cor. 13. It rates as one of the most beautiful pieces of writing in Scripture, if not in literature in general. It reflects at once the exalted theological ability of Paul and his understanding of what was the best in the Christian faith.

PROCEDURE

Have the group read at least 1 Cor. 13. If possible, have them read the first thirteen chapters and Acts 18:1–18. Share the background to the writing with the group before beginning the meditation.

Indicate a general outline of the meditation, that you will be taking the group down a path which leads into the ancient city, Ephesus. The group will be brought into a cottage on the outskirts of the city and will meet there the Apostle Paul who has been expecting them. As they enter, Paul will arise from a table where he is writing. He has just sketched the Hymn to Love. The guest will be invited to sit and to talk with Paul about the meaning of love. After some time, it will be time to leave.

After describing in brief the journey, have the group move to their places of meditation and lead them in the kind of relaxation exercise which is needed and then the following meditation.

THE MEDITATION

In your mind's eye you are standing on the top of a hill which overlooks a city down below you. Off in the distance you can see the outline of the harbor at which there are many Roman ships. The road beneath you is paved and reaches down toward the city. Begin making your way now down the road, noticing that there are many people coming and going.

The time of day is dusk. Evening is coming fast as you continue on your way. You are coming closer to the edge of town. As you approach the first few houses on the outskirts, notice that there is a path which goes off to the side and takes you away from the main thoroughfare. As you continue down this path, observe that it brings you to a small cottage which is set aside from the rest. Approach the entrance of the cottage slowly, in anticipation of your visit.

As you come to the doorway of the cottage, notice that the evening has come in its entirety and that there is a warm glow emanating from the windows and the door. As you stand for a moment at the door, looking into the cottage, notice that there is a man sitting inside. He is writing.

As you stand for a moment, he notices your presence and stops his writing and stands and comes to greet you. It is Paul and he has been expecting you. He invites you into the cottage. As you enter, be aware of the colors in the room and of the meager yet comfortable furnishings. Paul invites you to sit down facing him.

After the initial greetings, he mentions that he has just finished writing a hymn on love which he is including in the letter he is writing to his friends at Corinth.

Now you will have some time to visit with Paul, to talk with him about the Hymn to Love. Feel free to say what is on your mind and to wait for Paul also to speak his mind to you. This time is yours for that conversation.

(Pause four minutes)

Now it is time for your conversation with Paul to draw to a close. Knowing that you can return anytime you wish, make your way to the door of the cottage and say your farewells to Paul. After looking one last time about the room where you have been engaged in conversation, make your exit and start back up the path toward the outskirts of town.

As you make your way up the path, do not try to think on the meaning of the conversation you have just had. There is plenty of time for that later. Just be aware of the feelings that you have after having had the conversation.

Feel free as you make your way back to the top of the path to begin to come back into the normal state of consciousness at your own pace. Do not hurry, but come back at a relaxed pace, at whatever pace is comfortable for you.

Welcome back.

DEBRIEFING

As always, give the group the opportunity to say what first comes to their mind after the meditation. If the conversation does not go in any particular or fruitful direction, then begin to ask specific questions about the meditation. Ask about the imagery and the particular senses which seemed to be used during the meditation. Have them describe the room where Paul was and then have them describe Paul. Finally, have them describe the conversation and ask what it was that Paul had to say about love and how they felt about that. Ask what feelings they had which they could identify during the course of the meditation, particularly during and after the visit with Paul. Ask, then, what they may have learned from the meditation that was new. Were there any particular insights which were surprising or new?

Meditation: Meeting Our Prejudices

PURPOSE

To confess a prejudice and effect a response to it by means of studying the story of Peter and Cornelius.

BACKGROUND

It was difficult for the Jewish Christians to admit non-Jews into their midst as full-fledged Christians. In Acts 10 there is the story of Cornelius, a Gentile who worshipped at the synagogue but had not become a proselyte. He received a vision that his prayers had been answered and that he should send to Joppa for Simon Peter. At Joppa it is reported that Peter was praying on the housetop at noon. No doubt Peter was hungry. While he was waiting on the preparation of lunch, he went into a trance and saw a vision. The vision was perhaps the result of Peter's wrestling with the question of the Gentile mission. In any event, there are animals which Peter would not normally eat and a voice which commands him to eat. He refuses because he would not eat unclean beasts. The voice three times suggests that what God has called clean is not to be called unclean by Peter. The rest of the story in Acts 10 is a descriptive story indicating that the Spirit of God also descends on the Gentiles. The conclusion for Peter seems to be in Acts 10:28: "I need not tell you that a Jew is forbidden by his religion to visit or associate with a man of another race; yet God has shown me clearly that I must not call any man profane or unclean."

PROCEDURE

Ask the group to read Acts 10:1-11, 18. Take a brief time to indicate the nature of the problem for the Jew and the question of prejudice of one sort or another interfering with one's ministering. Indicate to the group that they will be asked to walk up to the housetop, and there they will see a sheet descending from Heaven, and on this sheet will be a symbolic representation of an object of prejudice toward which they should be responsive but are not. Do not decide now what that will be, but let it emerge in the meditation.

Lead the group in a relaxation exercise before beginning the meditation.

THE MEDITATION

Imagine you are standing alongside a house in the Palestinian port city of Joppa. You are dressed appropriately for the occasion. There before you is a staircase which leads up the side of the house to the flat roof. Begin to climb the stairway at a comfortable pace.

As you come to the top of the roof, notice the gentle breeze which is blowing in from the sea and notice also the colors of the tops of the trees and the color of the water as it extends out to the horizon. Notice that there are some boats in full sail coming into port. It is a busy day, but it is time for you to turn to prayer before your noon meal.

As you turn to a comfortable place to sit, notice that descending before you is a sheet or a tablecloth. As it comes down to you, observe an object or a number of objects sitting in the middle of the sheet. These objects are symbolic of some area of prejudice in your life, an area to which you have a responsibility of ministry, but which you may be resisting.

Notice your resistance as you are told to take the object in your hand, but a voice deep within you says to call nothing unworthy that God has called worthy. Take the object and look at it and become aware of the area of prejudice which you have been resisting as an authentic place of your ministering.

Replace the object on the sheet and let the sheet return to the place from whence it came. As you notice it ascending, hear your name being called from below. As you go downstairs, you will meet a person or persons who will have come to take you with them. They have come to take you to the place where you must perform the ministry you have been resisting.

As you go with this person come now to that place where you are to perform that ministry which you have been resisting because of your inner prejudice. Take some time now to work out that ministry in the midst of that place and as you perform it, notice that God has preceded you and that the Spirit is already present, that God is blessing this effort of yours. Take some time now to engage in this ministry to which God is calling you.

(Pause four minutes)

Now it is time for you to begin to leave this place where you have come to minister. You must leave because you must go now and tell others what you have learned. Begin now to leave that place and take whatever time you need to begin to come back to the level of awareness in which you normally are operating.

Welcome back.

DEBRIEFING

As always do not insist that anyone share unless they want to do so. The group should be free enough to know that they are welcome to talk but that there are not penalties for not doing so. However, try to be responsive and include that person who wants to talk but is reluctant to enter into the discussion without being prompted.

Ask specific and leading questions if the discussion does not normally develop. Ask if the imagery was clear. Ask what were some of the objects which were seen and what the meanings were. Ask what kinds of responses they had to the call to minister (remember that every Christian is a minister) in an area of resistance. Ask if the opportunity to see this area in the context of a meditation has given any new insights. Ask if this will make it possible to minister in this area.

7

Intercessory Meditation: Participating with God in the Healing Process

Intercessory prayer lies at the very heart of the Christian faith. The outpouring of the heart in concern for others is at the very center. In Georgia Harkness's words, "Take prayer for other persons out of the experience of the Christian, and a great deal goes with it. Jesus prayed for others as simply and naturally as he prayed for himself."[1] The fact, necessity, and importance of intercessory prayer are assumed throughout the New Testament.

It is often difficult for some Christians, however, to practice. Not that they don't have concern for others, but they have prayed before and not found the answers forthcoming. Often the response to the apparent disregard or inability of God to act leads to skepticism.

Others are put off by the implicit view of God contained in much intercessory prayer. Often the conception of God which our prayers affirm is not examined. For example, it seems that many have a "slot machine" God. Insert one prayer, pull the handle, and out pops the answer. This is an exaggeration, of course, but many persons have a view of God as being external, as existing "out there" somewhere, as if God existed over against his creation.

Implicit in such views of God is that prayer is a bringing to God's attention of something he would not otherwise know about. It is an absurd idea, but we do not stop to think how our prayers say this. Further, if God is out there and is unaware of what is going on, then we must bring his attention to matters and in some way coerce him to act. Much prayer, particularly intercessory prayer and prayer of petition is mere magic—an attempt to force God by some external means, our prayers, to do what needs to be done. Such an approach is a violation of the third commandment, which prohibits taking the name of God lightly.

A further unfortunate result of this kind of praying is that it tends to blunt our sense of responsibility for the world. If we have prayed for something to take place, for this person or that person, then we have in some sense discharged our responsibility toward that person, and we do not need to act any further. Again, we do not say this openly, but it is an implicit plank in the floor of our understanding of prayer.

If God is not a super delivery boy, if God is not out there, and if prayer is not getting in touch with a far removed supernatural being, then how shall we understand intercessory prayer?

Prayer as Participation with God

Prayer is not long-distance communication. It is not an exchange of information but "a union of persons in close and intimate relationship," as Norman Pittenger says. "The very essence of prayer, in Christian practice at least, is the intentional and attentive identification of our feeble human willing, purposing, and aspiring, with God's enormous loving care and activity."[2] Intercessory prayer is not our sending a message out there for God to act somewhere else. Intercessory prayer, particularly intercessory meditation, is the participation with God in the healing and creative process.

One of the most important passages in Scripture for me personally in terms of its having awakened me to my responsibility as a person in the world is the passage in Genesis where Adam names the animals: "So God formed out of the ground all the wild animals and all the birds of heaven. He brought them to the man to see what he would call them, and whatever the man called each living creature, that was its name. Thus the man gave names to all cattle, to the birds of heaven, and to every wild animal." (Genesis 2:19-20) To understand this story one must keep in mind what the Hebrews meant by the naming of the animals. A name was more than a simple designation for an object. For the Hebrew the name of something or someone revealed its nature. It was for this reason that the name of God was so sacred. A person's name therefore revealed his or her nature. When Adam named the animals, he was giving the nature to those particular animals. A cow was not a cow until Adam gave it the name; a lion was not a lion; a hawk was not a hawk. The meaning of this delightful story is, then, that human beings have been given the opportunity to participate in the creative process with God. We are not shut off from the creative process. We have been brought into it by God. And so we should not be disturbed if someday we hear that a person in a laboratory somewhere has been able to create life. When it happens it will be the case of a person exercising the God-given right of being a co-creator, of participating in the creative process.

To understand the human being as rightfully participating in the creative process has marvelous implications for intercessory meditations. We are not simply sending our messages outside, but we are actually participating within the process of creation and healing itself.

For some reasons many Christians want to resist this understanding. One sees it particularly in the matter of spiritual and psychic healing. Is it possible for a person to have the power actually to heal another person? For many it is simply an inconceivable thought. Many say, "Perhaps it could be that 'something' happens, but probably only in the case of a psychosomatic illness, i.e., not a real illness." Many of these same Christians would probably agree that Jesus was able to heal others, but that was a special case. And yet, what should we do with the passage in John in which Jesus says, "Believe me when I say that I am in the Father and the Father in me; or else accept the evidence of the deeds themselves. In truth, in very truth I tell you, he who has faith in me will do what I am doing; and he will do greater things still because I am going to the Father. Indeed anything you ask in my name I will do, so that the Father may be glorified in the Son. If you ask anything in my name I will do it." (John 14:11-14) This suggests that the power for healing which we describe as supernatural and therefore as belonging only to specially endowed and blessed persons may be more a natural human capacity which most of us have not developed. A look at some of the research being done in telepathy might prove helpful at this point.

Telepathic Communication and Intercessory Prayer

Contemporary psychic research suggests some interesting possibilities which will finally alter the way in which we think about the nature of the human being. We have tended to see human beings as being individuals who are basically unrelated to other human beings. Telepathic research is beginning to suggest that we need to re-think that model of the human being.

Several researchers working at the Dream Laboratory of the Maimonides Medical Center in Brooklyn have seen sufficient evidence of the influencing of dreams of carefully monitored subjects by outside telepathic senders in the laboratory to conclude that "the nature of the dynamic exchanges that it encompasses are far more subtle and complicated than current psychoanalytic and behavioral theory suggest."[3] Much more research will have to be done, but the evidence is beginning to grow that, as humans, we are more closely related than we have wanted to recognize.

In the Soviet Union there has been active psychic research going on for years. They have passed the point of trying to prove that ESP exists. They are now trying to discover what is happening and how to use what is happening. A fascinating series of reports on the ESP research in the Soviet Union is found in the work by the journalists Sheila Ostrander and Lynn Schroeder, *Psychic Discoveries Behind the Iron Curtain*. One report in particular is significant for intercessory meditation.[4]

Extended research has been carried out on telepathic communication between two Russian psychics, Karl Nikolaiev and Yuri Kamensky. Nikolaiev is particularly adept at "receiving" messages and Kamensky at "sending." One of the experiments put Nikolaiev in an isolated room where he was attached to several machines designed to monitor his bodily processes, including brain waves. Two rooms away in another shielded room, Kamensky was to send "messages" to Nikolaiev. The messages usually consisted of Kamensky's sending an image of some object by concentrating on the object and intentionally sending that concentrated image to Nikolaiev. Nikolaiev was to note when he became aware of receiving any telepathic communications. The success with which Nikolaiev could identify that he was receiving the communications and what he was receiving was far beyond the possibilities of chance, and it must be concluded that telepathic communications were taking place. What was astounding in the research, however, was that the brain waves of Nikolaiev, which were being recorded on the brain wave machine, the EEG, and being read by the scientist in another room, showed evidence of the telepathic message from one to five seconds before the subject consciously knew that he was in fact receiving the message.

Certainly we are not all Nikolaievs and Kamenskys and cannot expect to duplicate the feats of these "stars." Yet there are tentative conclusions which can be drawn from these and other stories. First, what Nikolaiev has is not a supernatural but a human power which he worked very hard at developing. As it happens, he decided he wanted to be a psychic when, as a youth, he saw a magician in a vaudeville act. He has succeeded admirably. He believes that we, as human beings, have capacities we simply have not developed. One of these areas is telepathic communication.

There are other fascinating parts to the Nikolaiev story. For example, the fact that his body "knew" he was receiving the message before "he" did suggests that one can receive such communications even if one is not aware of receiving the message. Other experiments between the two had Kamensky making Nikolaiev ill by sending images of a ship at sea, thereby causing seasickness from a distance. Understandably Nikolaiev does not care for these particular experiments, but they indicate the possibilities of interconnections between persons that we normally do not think of. It comes to mind that if a person can make a person sick by means of telepathic communication, can a person also not assist in the healing process? Why not?

Scientists have yet to discover the acceptable theory that will explain how such telepathy works. For the moment it doesn't matter. What does matter is that the interpersonal contact between persons is substantially different than our normal ways of thinking would have us believe. Perhaps we really are all one of another. Perhaps we can therefore participate in the healing process of others because we are intimately related as human beings. At the present time it seems that sympathetic subjects are more capable of sending and receiving telepathic communication, but it will not be long, I would guess, before we are going to discover that the human capacity for interaction with other persons is far greater than we have recognized.

John Killenger describes the amazing capacity of Uri Geller to distort metal objects by some force of his mind. Killenger wonders if there are not implications for our understanding of prayer: "If the parapsychologists are convincing in their evidence that people's minds can control the rolling of dice, then surely there are spiritual energies that can heal and bless. If there is indeed a power like Uri Geller's capable of distorting metal objects without visible force, then surely we cannot scoff at what religious people for centuries have called the power of prayer."[5] It is not any less significant for the Christian if much of the capacity turns out to be a human capacity and is not effected by praying to a God "out there" who works "over there." What it apparently suggests is that God has given human beings the capacity for participating in the creative process. In essence we are given the opportunity of naming the animals.

Intercessory Meditation

Intercessory meditations proceed on the basis of using imagery in praying for a person. If we use words in our intercessory prayers, it would seem to make as much sense then to use images. Let us use both our right brain and left brain in our intercessions.

One principle which is often cast as important in praying is that there be faith on the part of the person praying, that is, the person in prayer must believe that the praying makes a difference. It would seem to be the case that such is also true for those who would send telepathic messages and communications with any facility.

Believing that what is prayed for will be accomplished can have other possible meanings, however. In Mark the following words on prayer are found, as Jesus comments on the destruction of the fig tree: "Jesus answered them, 'Have faith in God. I tell you this: if anyone says to this mountain, "Be lifted from your place and hurled into the sea," and has not inward doubts, but believes that what he says is happening, it will be done for him. I tell you, then, whatever you ask for in prayer, believe that you have received it and it will be yours.' " (Mark 11:22-24)

The process of intercessory meditation is to visualize the person for whom you are praying in a state of health, or at least in the process of regaining health. This is in effect to pray believing that it is happening. In the meditative state one should concentrate on the object of the meditation as if it had already happened. When we find our daughter during one of her occasional asthma attacks, we visualize her being relaxed and her lungs opening up and breathing normally. My wife will add to that the visual imagery of our daughter dancing with joy, which she would not do without her lungs being able to breathe freely. By use of visualization, we pray, believing that it has already happened.

Bob Keck, who introduced me to this particular approach, sounds a word of caution for the person who practices this kind of prayer: "To put our skills of concentration on the *problem* may only magnify the problem; a better way would be to visualize a happy and successful and well person, or at least a person in the process of healing."⁶ After all, what one is praying for the other person is health and not a sickness.

It would seem that this kind of intercessory meditation would be particularly fruitful between those persons who are close to one another, that is, a relative or close friend. I believe we will likely discover before much longer that the capacity to send such messages of health can be directed also with benefit to those who do not know us or expect such. I am convinced that we have been given the capacity for enhanced interaction between persons and that we ought to learn to develop that capacity.

Interceding for Oneself

We can also enlist the intercessory meditation in behalf of our own health in an imaginative approach to our own well-being. After all, if there is such a thing as psychosomatic illness that we bring on to ourselves, why not psychosomatic health and healing?

There are numerous examples of this kind of self-healing being instigated by means of visualization. One of the more dramatic authentic stories I am personally aware of is the story of Bob Keck, Director of New Wineskins: A Center for Christian Research and

Development in Columbus, Ohio. He has told his story in person across the country and recently in an article in *The Christian Ministry.*[7]

Bob had developed a severe back pain because of polio, a broken back, and corrective surgery. The pain became so bad that he was not able to stand for more than five or ten minutes. He found that drugs were becoming less and less effective. In a state of desperation he finally found an answer to the pain by imaginatively dispatching it in a meditation. He did this visually before the pain itself could reach his brain and be registered there as pain. That experience led Bob to develop a synthesis of several disciplines including biofeedback, transpersonal psychology, meditation, imagery and Christian prayer into what he calls Meditative Prayer.

There are other examples of the use of imagery to enhance the healing process in persons. There are psychotherapeutic approaches which make use of imagery, as, for example, in the treatment of phobias. In this process a person, in a state much like a meditative state, visualizes an increasingly difficult series of acts until the major hold of the phobia is to all intents and purposes broken.[8] I have little difficulty seeing this as a form of intercessory meditation since it is an act of participating in the creative process by means of a God-given capacity for enhancing health and well-being.

Others use the imagery within a distinctly Christian context. Ruth Carter Stapleton, in her book, *The Gift of Inner Healing,*[9] describes a variety of experiences in which she leads persons in need of healing through imaginative meditations in which the persons enter into a dialogue with Jesus at a significant point. Based upon the psychological insights of Jung and Hugh Missledine and using meditative techniques in conjunction with her particular Christian approach, Ruth Stapleton teaches a method whereby persons can learn to enlist their inner being in the process of healing.

For me the most eminently practical use of this kind of intercessory meditation occurs when a migraine headache approaches. Although I have only an occasional bout with migraine, it is enough to create a fair amount of anxiety when I suspect one is forthcoming. Fortunately I have the classical migraine which gives me a warning of about twenty minutes before the headache itself begins. By means of the biofeedback training and the meditative disciplines which I have learned over the past two years, I can fully abort the onset of a migraine headache by becoming very deeply relaxed and visualizing my hands soaking in hot water. The fact is, this is a physiological and psychological technique which works. Is it an intercessory meditation? This is participating in the healing process as God has intended for us to do. Not long ago I experienced the beginning of such a headache. I pushed back from my desk and entered into a meditative state and visualized my hands in a hot whirlpool. A few minutes of the practice and the headache had been aborted. By all rights I should have been sent home with a terrible, incapacitating headache, but instead I was left with a whole day in which to work. I was never so aware of life as a gift as I was that day. Everything I accomplished was a result of grace and was received as a gift.

Intercessory Meditation and Responsibility

Two concluding remarks seem in order on the matter of intercessory meditation. First, in any kind of prayer, but especially in intercessory prayer, we ought never to decide that we have done all that was necessary when we have prayed. This seems a particular serious temptation and one to be avoided at all costs. Whenever one prays, one should become part of the answer of the prayer. We have not done everything if we stop with the prayer. The prayer itself ought to make us more responsible and aware of the needs of others and thereby increase our own personal responses to persons for whom we pray.

Another variation of that same warning is worth making. Whenever we use the intercessory meditation, we always use it in the context of good medical procedure. If our daughter has an asthma attack and a fit of coughing, we give her cough medicine and a meditation. If she has a high fever, we give her aspirin and a meditation. The skeptic will say that the medicine does the work and the meditation makes us feel better. We don't think so, but we do think that God intends for us to use all the resources that are at our command. For us this means taking the appropriate medicine. We never set the intercessory meditation over against the practice of good medicine.

A second warning relates to the necessity of being responsible in what we ask for. It is fashionable in Christian circles to pray for the recovery of a person and to tack on the escape clause, "If it be thy [God's] will." It is important to discover God's will and to pray in accorance with that, but it is not appropriate to intercede for someone and not to take that question of God's will into consideration beforehand. We are presumptuous to assume that we know what is best for anyone, even recovery from illness. This does not mean that we do not then act; rather, it means that we attempt to act responsibly. It is somewhat dangerous to engage in the intercessory meditation and attach the escape clause, so that the person will be able to use what they need. When we are engaging in the practice of such communications, we are being irresponsible if we do not weigh the possible side effects and dangers beforehand. The meditative process is itself neutral and does not have the capacity to filter out whether or not this person should or should not receive the help we are sending, whether it be serious healing or only "energy." The point is, again, that we act responsibly, not that we don't act.

As Norman Pittenger points out, when we engage in prayer we learn the will of God and purify our motives and widen our vision:

> By the aligning of our desires with God's purpose, by the identification of our will with his, we may be free from immediate self-concern for interests and objects that are of the sort to interfere with our truly becoming the selves which we know to be for our best fulfillment—and this, be it remembered, always in community with

our fellows. At the heart of prayer, interpreted in this fashion, is a rejoicing in the sheer goodness and love of God, with thanksgiving for all that we receive "from his hands," and with a renewed dedication to His service. Inevitably this will lead to a recognition of our own failing, defects, and distortions of sense of petition and intercession.[11]

Meditation: Intercession

PROCEDURE

Mention to your group that the purpose of this meditation is intercessory and bring to their attention the thoughts of this chapter. Perhaps the group members will want to share concerns with each other so that others can be included in the meditation. When our meditation group does this, we usually say something about the person so that it is not a total stranger for whom we are interceding. This meditation will use a room with a chair in which the person can be sitting, bathed in light. Variations on this include having the person outside in a pleasant place or in a place where the person or persons would normally be in a state of health.

Lead the group in a relaxation exercise before beginning the meditation.

THE MEDITATION

In your mind's eye, you now see before you a room in the middle of which is sitting a chair. The chair is bathed in light. Let this light symbolize for you the healing power of God. Picture the person for whom you are praying. Have the person in a state of health or wholeness. You will have a few minutes to concentrate on this person and on any others whom you want to include.

(Pause four minutes)

Now it is time for you to draw your meditation to a close. Knowing that you can return here at anytime, begin to bring yourself back to the state of normal awareness.

DEBRIEFING

Allow whatever questions emerge to come from the group. Ask what kinds of imagery the members used and how they felt during the meditation. At the end of the session encourage the group to find some appropriate means of becoming the answer to their own prayer, of becoming an agent of healing in the life of the person for whom they have just prayed.

8

Christian Meditation in a World of Action

The great temptation for those who practice Christian meditation is to become so involved in meditations and in the cultivation of the inner life that they lose sight of the world of action in which they are living. The inner world is a fascinating, exciting, and indeed an enticing world. It could become very enjoyable for a person to stay in the inner world so much that the outer world was of little concern.

There is a subtle temptation presenting itself to the pilgrim of the inner life, particularly when the spiritual world is described as the "real" world. It is the temptation which is often present in the practice of spirituality and Christian devotion.

Not too long ago I was in conversation with a friend about a mutual concern of ours, namely, the world food crisis. We were trying to think of some ways to involve persons in her congregation in some study and action groups centered about the concerns of world hunger. Much to my surprise, the main reason she offered for the lack of interest in the issue locally was that the active persons in her church were mostly interested in meditative prayer and their energies were going into that area.

What a pity! Apparently that congregation had persons who were either interested in feeding the hungry or in feeding the spiritually hungry. For some reason it had developed into an either/or situation. If you were involved in the hunger crisis, you did not have time for, or did not need to be involved in, the meditative prayer groups, and if you were practicing meditative prayer then you did not find yourself involved in working in the hunger crisis.

This either/or situation was not unfamiliar, but I could not help wondering why it had to be so often one way or the other. Why not both ways? Why not Christian meditation *and* involvement in the world?

One reason this division between the practice of personal piety and active involvement in the world so often occurs is that we are not careful enough to stress the two approaches as equally necessary dimensions of the Christian life. "Quite frequently," as Karl Hertz says, "they are treated as exclusive alternatives; so we are presumably forced to choose between the cultivation of certain religious virtues, prayer and meditation, personal holiness before God, on the one hand, and social involvement, compassionate activity and witness in behalf of the neighbor, prophetic demands for social justice, on the other hand."[1]

The debate has often raged in Christian history as to which life is the more important, the active or the contemplative. Many theologians asserted the contemplative path was the better way. The fourteenth century mystic, Meister Eckhart, wrote, "The genuine word of eternity is spoken only in that eternity of the man who is himself a wilderness."[2] The hermit of Hampole, Richard Rolle, assured his readers that "It is known that contemplative life is worthier and fuller of need than active life."[3]

Since it was not uncommon to find similar assertions coupled with the notion that the contemplative was the one person who could reach perfection, it was not surprising that anything that was not the highly spiritual life was of lesser importance. If the active life is less than perfection, then it only makes sense for serious Christians to opt out of worldly involvement. In the Middle Ages, the spiritual person was one who had renounced the world and had taken up the religious life of monk or cleric.

Such a view is inevitable if the Christian sees the present world as a vale of tears, a hindrance to true Christian living. If only we were not tied down to the body, to the flesh, to this world. As the hymn says, "This world is not my home./ I'm just a'passin' through./ My treasures are laid up/ Somewhere beyond the blue."

In this frame of mind the serious business of the Christian is understood in terms of spiritual matters such as prayer and worship. When it is carried to an extreme, persons become hermits and sometimes even shut themselves off from the normal flow of human life. At its worst this view sees other persons as an interference in one's own spiritual life. The danger also exists that the practice of spiritual disciplines such as meditation could simply blind one to the world in which one is living. As much as I am attracted to the person of the pilgrim in *The Way of the Pilgrim,* at one point he becomes too engrossed in his own personal piety: "I have become a sort of half-conscious person. I have no cares and no interests. The fussy business of the world I would not give a glance to. The one thing I wish for is to be alone, and all by myself to pray, to pray without ceasing; and doing this, I am filled with joy."[4] Admirable as this may sound in terms of its devoted practice of prayer, I cannot personally believe that God desires half-conscious persons who shut themselves off from the world. After all, God loved this world so much that he gave his Son, and this Son was hardly characterized as one who went about in a half-conscious state, looking only for the opportunity to get away and to pray. Indeed, he was even called a glutton and carouser, hardly the characteristics of a spiritual narcissist. We hear echoes of this spiritual narcissism, however, when we hear the church member saying, "Why doesn't the pastor stick to preaching the Gospel and stop fooling around in politics?" There are endless variations on this theme, but it is all too commonly expressed.

The Spiritual Life and the Active Life in Scripture

It is not surprising that both the active and the contemplative life are stressed in the Scriptures. A brief look at some of the examples of biblical spirituality, devotion, and practice will help us to formulate a basis for the practice of Christian meditation in the world of action.

Perhaps the primary teaching on the subject of contemplation and meditation is drawn from the story of Mary and Martha:

> While they were on their way Jesus came to a village where a woman named Martha made him welcome in her home. She had a sister, Mary, who seated herself at the Lord's feet and stayed there listening to his words. Now Martha was distracted by her many tasks, so she came to him and said, 'Lord, do you not care that my sister has left me to get on with the work by myself? Tell her to come and lend a hand.' But the Lord answered, 'Martha, Martha, you are fretting and fussing about so many things; but one thing is necessary. The part Mary has chosen is best; and it shall not be taken away from her.' (Luke 10:38–42)

The point of this story is clear: Mary, representing the quiet, relaxed attention to the presence of the Lord, is the preferred figure.

The contrast is striking. Martha welcomes Jesus and the disciples into the home but then proceeds to become so involved in the preparation of the table that she simply fails to be present with them, to enjoy their presence in her home. What Martha is doing is important, but she has become so engrossed in the busyness of her tasks that she is not benefiting from the presence of the Lord in her home. Mary, on the other hand, sits quietly at Jesus' feet, drinking in the full benefits of his presence. "One thing is necessary," says Jesus. The other things can wait for a while, but now Mary has chosen the better way.

It was very natural for those who were drawn to the contemplative life to exalt the image of Mary in this story. Clearly she is here presented as the spiritual person in contrast to the figure of Martha whose preoccupation with the things of the world, however necessary these occupations may be, prevents her full enjoyment of the presence and person of Jesus. The great truth here for Christians is that if we would be authentically close to God, we must be prepared to put aside for a time the scurrying about, the preparing of the table, the concerns for the external matters before us, and simply be present with the Lord. All too often we, as Christians, are concerned about what we must do, when the essence of the Christian life should first be understood as being, not doing. It is what the Quaker Thomas Kelly speaks of as the "sense of Presence." One "centers down" and lives life with "singleness of eye, from a holy Center where the breath and stillness of Eternity are heavy upon us and we are wholly yielded to Him.'"[5] In this experience "one walks in the world yet above the world as well, giddy with the height, with feather tread, with effortlessness and calm security, meeting the daily routine, yet never losing the sense of Presence." [6]

One does not stop with the story of Mary, however, when reading the Scripture, and we should be careful not to exalt her to a place where she could well become all there is to Christian life. As a student of church history, I am fascinated by the stories throughout the church's history of heretics who glimpsed a truth of the faith and turned their understanding of that truth into an absolute, thereby shutting out an equally important affirmation which should temper the absolute. The fact is, social concern is also a serious concern of Scripture, and to be entirely correct, we should speak of the inward life and the outward concern at precisely the same moment. They are two sides of the one coin. The Christian life is not to be turned in on itself but is to be directed outward toward the neighbor. The natural movement, after having come into the encounter of the Divine Presence, is to go out into the world. We are to love God *and* our neighbor.

There are so many biblical stories which point to the way back into active involvement in the world. For the record, after a decisive encounter with God, a person usually is not told to go and pray for the world; rather, by command and example, the disciple is to go *into* the world. At the burning bush, Moses encounters the God of Israel, and he is told to go back to Egypt to lead the children of Israel out of bondage. Elijah encounters God at the cave and is told to go back and to anoint the future kings of Israel and Syria. The work of Moses and of Elijah was essentially political in the performance of these tasks. For Moses to lead Israel out of bondage, he had to enter into a contest with the powerful political leader of Egypt. For Elijah to anoint the future kings of Israel and Syria (which didn't even worship the God of Israel!), he was engaging in political activity which, in effect, brought about palace revolutions. What a thought! Elijah encounters his God and is sent to get involved in the political life of two different countries, even to the point of precipitating a revolution! These stories are startling in their impact. The disciple is led through the experience with God into political involvement. This is an exceptionally clear illustration of the fact that encounter with God and political activity are compatible. Indeed, the one leads into the other.

The story of Amos, the prophet of eighth century Israel, provides some valuable insights for understanding the importance of social responsibility and involvement by the person of God. Amos came to prophesy in Israel during the reign of Jeroboam II. To the casual observer, Israel was prospering, both economically and religiously. Business must have been great. Yet not all was well, because the poor were suffering under an oppressive economic system which allowed the rich to become richer at the expense of the poor. Amos was not a professional prophet but a somewhat poor herdsman and "dresser of sycamore figs" from Tekoa in Judah. It is clear that his own economic situation allowed him to identify with the poor who were being oppressed in Israel. Amos had a view of God as sovereign God, the Lord of Hosts "at whose touch the earth heaves, and all who dwell on it wither." (Amos 9:5, see also 4:13) Apparently Amos was able to carry his view of God as sovereign Lord to its rightful conclusion. If God is the Lord of all the earth, then he must also be the Lord of social institutions and of relationships, and it was into this milieu that Amos brought his word from the Lord.

Amos did not just come into Israel to preach about religion. He did have some words to say about religion, mostly to the effect that Yahweh was not pleased by the practice of religious exercises: "I hate, I spurn your pilgrim-feasts; I will not delight in your sacred ceremonies. When you present your sacrifices and offerings I will not accept them, nor look on the buffaloes of your shared-offerings. Spare me the sound of your songs; I cannot endure the music of your lutes." (Amos 5:21-23) It was not for lack of religion that Amos was in Israel prophesying the imminent downfall of Israel. There was plenty of religion, too much in fact. There was not, however, enough justice: "Let justice roll on like a river and righteousness like an everflowing stream." (Amos 5:24) The fact is, justice had disappeared from the courts and the poor were being oppressed by a fat, luxury class who "loll on beds inlaid with ivory . . . feasting on lambs from the flock and fatted calves." (Amos 6:4) These were a people who had become soft, and who had assumed that because they were God's people and had always worshipped Yahweh, that they were always going to be blessed by him. Amos, however, saw another vision. He saw that God was just, and that he demanded justice in society, and that unless the wrongs in the society were changed, there would only be destruction for Israel: "Seek good and not evil, that you may live, that the LORD the God of Hosts may be firmly on your side, as you say he is. Hate evil and love good; enthrone justice in the courts; it may be that the LORD the God of Hosts will be gracious to the survivors of Joseph." (Amos 5:14–15)

It is clear from the example of the prophet Amos that God is not only concerned about personal piety, indeed not only about religion, but that God is also greatly concerned about the social and political order. The sovereign Lord is concerned about such matters as justice in the courts, unjust business transactions and perjury. As James Gustafson reminds us, God is the Lord of human life altogether. He is the Lord of the concentrations of power in institutions and the particular offices that men fill in them. God is concerned not only about the Father and the Son but also about the relationship between the father and the son. If God is the Lord of all, then he is not only Lord over individuals, and is not only concerned about the conversion of the individual, but is Lord over society's institutions and seeks the conversion of those institutions. "Excessive concentration on God's will and way for persons too often loses sight of God's will and way for the impersonal, and shrinks the scope of God's sovereignty and in turn the scope of human Christian responsibility."[7]

The example of Amos suggests that Israel had some difficulty in understanding appropriately what it meant to be the "Chosen People of God." It is clear that they saw it as some sort of privilege and interpreted it often as meaning that God was somehow obligated to bless them because he had chosen them. Yahweh, especially as represented by the prophets of Israel, saw it another way. It was not to privilege that Israel was called but to responsibility, a fact which Israel constantly had difficulty remembering Israel was to be the representative of Yahweh in the world, and therefore more, not less, was required of her.

Eventually both Israel and Judah fell. Israel was dispersed, and Judah was carried into exile. Out of the exile and in the post-exilic time, Judaism underwent a change which is of significance for the Christian's understanding of action in the world.

When Israel went into exile, she lost most of the tangible signs which had provided a focus for determining her identity. The temple was destroyed, and they had been separated from Jerusalem, the center of their worship and government. When they returned to Jerusalem, they were not the same nation they had been when they had been forced to leave. In fact, they were not a nation at all. It was due to the efforts of leaders such as Ezra and Nehemiah that Judaism began to form as the religion we Christians knew it to be in the days of the early church. In order to maintain its identity in the face of tremendous pressures from the outside, Judaism developed as a particularistic religion, essentially drawing a circle around herself and shutting everyone else out. In this way Judaism was guaranteed of continued existence even though the nation Israel did not exist as before. The Law particularly was invaluable in providing the religious identity for a narrow and particularistic religion. Yet this was not all there was to Judaism; there was a minority of those who returned to Jerusalem who represented another alternative, one of particular significance for the rise of the church.

The second alternative found its manifestation in the writings of prophets like Isaiah of Babylon, or Deutero-Isaiah, and Jonah. It was not necessary to see Judaism as a particularistic religion which had the responsibility of maintaining the distinctive qualities of God's chosen people at all costs. Another tradition, the Servant tradition, was also available. The notion of the Servant which is especially recorded in Chapters 42-66 of Isaiah saw Israel as being chosen not for privilege but for service: "Here is my servant, whom I uphold, my chosen one in whom I delight, I have bestowed my spirit upon him, and he will make justice shine on the nations." (Isa. 42:1) In this tradition, God calls Israel to be the Servant of Yahweh: "I, the LORD, have called you with righteous purpose and taken you by the hand; I have formed you, and appointed you to be a light to all peoples, a beacon for the nations, to open eyes that are blind, to bring captives out of prison, out of the dungeons where they lie in darkness." (Isa. 42:6–7) The great majority of those who returned did not adopt this option, but it was a live option. The story of Jonah, the reluctant prophet to the Gentiles of Nineveh, continues the theme of servanthood. Israel, as the people of Yahweh, the God of Israel, was to be his representative to all nations, that is, to the Gentiles, hence to *all* the world. It was a calling for responsibility, not for privilege. It is this tradition which I believe the Church of Jesus Christ is called to fulfill.

Christian Responsibility for the World

Jesus himself was greatly influenced by the tradition of the Servant of Yahweh. His own conception of ministry and mission was shaped and informed by it. His own disciples did not understand, but Jesus resisted the attempts to become the king of a particularistic nation, choosing rather to understand his mission in terms of the Servant motif. When he sat down, in the synagogue, he read from the book of Isaiah and announced, "Today . . . in your very hearing this text has come true." (Luke 4:21)

If the Christians are to be faithful to this vision of Jesus and his followers as servants, they will have to rediscover what it means to be the representatives of God in the world. We are chosen not for privilege but for servanthood. We are God's representatives in the world. James Gustafson speaks of the Christian's role as that of the deputy, that is, we are deputized by God to serve him in the world.[8]

What does it mean to be God's deputy in the world? It suggests that Christians have a special responsibility to God. Because of their acknowledgement of him, their confession of him, they are authorized by him and obligated to him for a life of service in the world. As Gustafson says, "One is not usually deputized in general; to be a deputy is to have an assigned task, it is to execute the will of the one who authorizes within the sphere of his authority."[9] The special deputyship of the Christian community is that of the servant, and this grows out of God's choosing us. It is not enough to be religious, to seek spiritual growth, admirable as these qualities may seem to be. Rather, we must live out our faith in the role of the Servant, and it must be recognized that this is not all to be understood as an easy or comfortable task. We should remember that it was said of the Servant in Isaiah and revealed in the Servanthood of Jesus that to be true to one's calling of Servanthood is costly: "He was afflicted, he submitted to be struck down and did not open his mouth; he was led like a sheep to the slaughter, like a ewe that is dumb before the shearers. Without protection, without justice, he was taken away; and who gave a thought to his fate, how he was cut off from the world of living men, stricken to the death for my people's transgression?" (Isa. 53:7-8) If this is true of the Master, will it not also be true for those who follow him?

For the Christian to fail to take seriously his or her responsibility for living out the Christian faith in the world of action is in some very real sense to deny the Incarnation. Part of what the Incarnation means is that God has decisively entered into human history in a personal way and has chosen to reveal himself amongst human beings, indeed, in the life of one particular human being. As followers of the Christ, we are not to follow slavishly his external dress. It does mean that we are to work among the press of humanity to free them from the oppressiveness of dehumanizing social systems. Remembering that the Sabbath was made for human beings and not vice versa, we are to commit ourselves to serving persons and not just religious systems. We must remember that God is *still* at work in history, and wherever we see God working amidst political and social structures to humanize and to heal humanity, we should be there. And wherever we see the inhumanity of persons and structures toward other humans, there we are to become directly involved to serve as God's deputies in bringing the word of God's concern for all of the world.

On one occasion it is reported that the disciples of John the Baptizer approached Jesus and asked if he were the one for whom they were waiting or should they seek another. Jesus answered them by pointing to his activity in the world: "Go, and tell John what you have seen and heard: how the blind recover their sight, the lame walk, the lepers are made clean, the deaf hear, the dead are raised to life, the poor are hearing the good news—and happy is the man who does not find me a stumbling block." (Luke 7:22–23) Jesus chose this means of his healing activity to be the test of his mission in the world. It is also to be our task, and if we remember the passage in John 14, we must know that we are to do even more remarkable wonders than he. We are to become involved in the world as healers and as peacemakers.

What, then, do we learn from reading the Scriptures about our role in the world? We learn that God is the God who cares, who is close to his people, and who sends his agents into the oppressive systems of the day to bring a word of liberation. More than this, God expects his followers to become directly involved in the freeing of others from their bondage. We learn also that God is the sovereign Lord, and that this must mean that God is Lord over institutions and relationships, or else we are limiting the sovereignty of God. It must mean, then, that God expects his followers, his agents, his servants, to minister also to relationships, to social institutions and to political entities. Finally, we have seen that God has come to us as Servant and that if we are to be true to this vision, then we are to choose not the safe way which protects our own identity, whether of religion or country, but that we are to move outward in service to all humankind.

There are also paradigms of Christian activity in the world available to us in the history of the church. Others before us have seen the vision of God's work in the world, and we should understand that one's commitment to God, one's spirituality, and one's devotion to God does not end without moving beyond self into the world. As we endeavor to learn from stories in the Bible and do so by reliving the story in our own lives, so too might we profit from adapting the motif of other Christians to our own situations. The stories of other Christians can and should inform us as we write our own stories.

Spiritual Christians in a World of Action

The image of the spiritual person whose spirituality leads into, rather than out of, the world occurs often in the history of the church. Francis of Assisi, the founder of the Franciscans, certainly stands as an example of one committed to Christ. It was not a commitment which avoided the world, however much we moderns might look askance upon Francis's devotion to Lady Poverty.

When Jesus the Christ called Francis he told him to "Go and repair my church." It was not just interpreted as a call to build up the spiritual church. "It never occurred to Francis that Christ was asking anything other than the actual repairing of churches that were falling into ruin. So he ran from San Damiano and set about collecting stones to rebuild crumbling churches. He would start with San Damiano itself. His whole mind and energy were now focused almost fanatically on this one project."[10] Francis's devotion to Christ was so nearly total that it is said that his hands and feet bore the stigmata, the marks of the crucified Christ. This is not just a story about the spirituality of Francis but a symbol of Francis' involvement in the world. The hands and the feet symbolize work and movement among people, and this is what Francis symbolizes. He was one who wore the Gospel as a witness among all people. He spent literally hours in prayer, but his movement was among people. Although he did not seek and did not have power, he moved among those who did as an outgrowth of his witness. Much more could and should be said, but the image of the movement is there: from spiritual experience into the world.

Another paradigm of this movement from spirituality to involvement in the world is Martin Luther. There likely has never been another person who knocked so hard on the gates of Heaven seeking salvation. And once he was discovered by Grace and freed by his faith in the Gracious God, his whole life characterizes a movement from spirituality into the world. Indeed, one sees in his movement from the cloister into the rough and tumble world of

German and European church/power politics the symbolic movement of one who has encountered the Christ and has not been left alone thereafter. Martin Luther was one of those decisive figures in the history of western civilization, one whose life has made all the difference in the world for those who came after him. Would, or could, the impact have been so great if Martin had been content merely with the discovery of the graciousness of God for himself?

A contemporary figure who represents both personally and conceptually the movement of spirituality in the world is the contemplative from the Saharan desert, Carlo Carretto. He reports that the call of Christ has taken him to the desert where he would dearly love to stay, for it is in the desert that he can truly pray to and love God. He has discovered, however, that his contemplation cannot be isolated from the needs of real people. The desert is necessary, that is, solitude and a space where one can encounter the living God must be experienced, but the Christian life does not stop there. He writes:

> The desert is not the final stopping place. It is a stage on the journey. Because, as I told you, our vocation is contemplation in the streets.
>
> For me, this is quite costly. The desire to continue living here in the Sahara forever is so strong that I am already suffering in anticipation of the order that will certainly come.
>
> Contemplation in the streets. A good phrase, but very demanding.
>
> Certainly it would be easier and more pleasant to stay here in the desert. But God doesn't seem to want that.[11]

The movement that God calls for is one that pauses in the desert, in the place of solitude and quiet, but which then moves into the streets. What particularly concerns me in introducing persons to the practice of Christian meditation is that they do not become so involved in the interior life that they forget that the external life is also very real and very important. Prayer, Christian meditation, and worship of God does not cut one off from the real problems of the world. "Far from amounting to a surrender of involvement in social change, the commitment to a religious, worshipful, contemplative way of life is a profoundly political act with specific implications for everything from prison reform to exploitative trade practices," insists James Carroll.[12] As Christians we must not only be content with enhancing our own Christian devotion or content with saving others' souls. When a contemporary evangelist like Billy Graham makes a distinction between the Old Testament prophet and the New Testament evangelist, he is making a distinction which does not exist in the Scripture. Worse than this, he is destroying the integrity of the Christian life. If we are to be practitioners of Christian meditation, then let us practice our meditation in the streets.

Meditation: The Burning Bush

PURPOSE

To meet God, as Moses did, at the burning bush and to discover there the God who is near to his people and to receive a commission from God to carry back into the world.

BACKGROUND

The Children of Israel were in bondage in Egypt. At one time the descendants of Abraham, Isaac and Jacob had enjoyed the favor of the Egyptian government and had prospered in Egypt. A change in government had precipitated the downfall of the Children of Israel in Egypt. The Scripture says, "Then a new king ascended the throne of Egypt, one who knew nothing of Joseph." (Exod. 1:8) The bondage was severe, as it is recorded in the early chapters of

Exodus, and as far as we can tell it was not a religious bondage but a political one; that is, the Children of Israel were not prohibited from practicing their religion, but they were restricted in their freedom of movement and forced into labor camps for the king.

Moses grew up as both an Egyptian and a Hebrew. He was publicly acknowledged as an Egyptian prince, but inwardly he identified with the people of Israel. He had been forced to leave Egypt because of his identification with the oppressed people, and he now found himself in the wilderness of Sinai, tending the flocks of his father-in-law Jethro, the priest of Midian. It was on the side of the mountain of God, Mount Horeb or Sinai, that God appeared to Moses in a burning bush. The burning bush was truly a wonderful sight which captured Moses' attention, and out of that bush came the voice of God, the God of the oppressed people back in Egypt whom Moses had left in fleeing for his life.

We must be careful not to become too enamoured of the burning bush. It was of no particular significance in itself. It was important only as the place where Moses met God, and it symbolizes the place where God comes to a particular person for a particular encounter. It is a sign of God's presence and nothing more. It is important to recognize that Moses never alluded to the burning bush when he was seeking authority for his message, and the bush is never mentioned again in the Scriptures. After all, when we get to any place we are going, we forget all about the signs which led us there. In any event, the bush only represents a dramatic picture of the place where God encounters a human being in a personal way; that is, God speaks to Moses—and conversation is an intensely human, personal form of communication. It is important, I think, to recognize that when God comes to a person, he essentially humanizes the person through conversation and dialogue.

Moses sees the bush which is not consumed and wonders what is going on. God calls to Moses out of the bush and reveals himself as the God of the people in bondage, the God of Abraham, Isaac and Jacob. This is important: God is the God of a people, indeed, of a people in bondage. God says to Moses, "I have indeed seen the misery of my people in Egypt. I have heard their outcry against their slave-masters. I have taken heed of their sufferings, and have come down to rescue them from the power of Egypt, and to bring them up out of that country." (Exod. 3:7–8) This statement tells us a great deal about God. He says, "I have *seen*. . . . I have *heard*. . . . I have *taken heed*. . . . and have *come down*." The God whom Moses encounters is a near God, not an aloof God. This is not a God who is far off and removed but a God who sees his people in bondage, notes their misery, and comes down to them to free them from their oppression.

There is no doubt much more that could be said about this encounter, but I think it would all be elaboration on this theme. God is a caring God, a near God who comes to his people. God is not content merely with Moses' praise and adoration in what must have been an intense religious experience at the burning bush. Moses is not charged to build a Church of the Burning Bush for the purpose of worshipping the God who is capable of such marvelous wonders and miracles. Instead, Moses is charged with going back into Egypt to lead the children of Israel out of bondage. This is an essentially political act that Moses will be engaged in. He will become an agent of liberation. All of Moses' complaints and excuses were set aside by God, and Moses was sent back into Egypt.

The story of the burning bush can become for us the opportunity to encounter the personal God who commissions his servants to go into the world to lead those out of bondage who are oppressed. This is the purpose of meditation in the streets. We meet God in the solitude of the desert, that is, in the quiet of our own worship time. We are not left to worship alone, however. Instead, God has an agenda for us which involves activity in the political and social world "out there." Our commitment as Christians is a commitment within the context of a world of action, and God sends us out to engage in concrete acts of liberation. The point I am trying to make is that God does not only want his people to be "religious" and to engage in "religious acts of worship and praise." There is no sharp cleavage driven between the sacred and the secular by God. I believe that wherever there are persons in bondage, whether oppressed by religious or governmental authorities or even by one's own conscience, there God intends to send agents of liberation. I believe that wherever oppression is being challenged and lifted, God is already at work, and it is our challenge to join in the lifting of those bonds, whatever they might be, again whether social, religious or political.

In the intensely religious experience, our sensitivity is to be sharpened; we are to hear the call of God and we are to respond by going into the world of action. It is this which we can experience at the burning bush.

PROCEDURE

After the story has been read and the historical and biblical background has been shared with the group, then the group shall find a comfortable place where they can comfortably hear the leader, who leads first in a relaxation exercise and then offers the following meditation or a more suited variation.

THE MEDITATION

In your mind's eye you are standing on the side of a hill somewhere in the Sinai desert. You are dressed appropriately for the place and time. On your feet are sandals and in your hand is a staff.

It is nearing evening time. It has been a long day. You have been tending sheep. All around you are the sights and sounds of scores of sheep. They are settling down for the night which is coming. Knowing that the care of the sheep is in the good hands of your helpers, begin making your way up to the crest of the hill just ahead of you.

128

As you make it to the crest of the hill take time to look out into the distance and see that the sun is descending just beyond the mountains in the distance. Be aware of the colors of the sky as the sun disappears. Note the shapes of the mountains and the colors which are apparent to you in the oncoming dusk.

It is not uncomfortable where you are. There is a gentle breeze blowing, rustling your hair and your clothes. Be aware of the breeze as it softly skims across your face. A sense of contentment, of peace with the world, and of unity with the Creator pervades your being. These have been important days, for you have had the opportunity to let your mind wander back to the place where you have come from, to know that all that has gone into making you who you are has prepared you to be an agent of God's work in the world. There is something which you are uniquely suited to accomplish and you are becoming aware that God's work is to be done by you in a particular place and time, using the special qualities and capacities which God has given you. You are God's deputy.

Now, with the awareness that all is well taken care of in camp, begin making your way down the hill before you, away from the camp, following slowly the path before you. Feel the ground under your feet. Look out to the side and note the bushes and shrubbery growing there. Perhaps there are blossoms on the bushes and trees. Do you see some birds flying through the evening air, or do you hear some insects joining into a symphony of praise?

Continue on your way, gently descending on the path before you. Now as you continue on your way, look off to the side and notice that there is a glow in the distance. Stop your descent and look more closely. You see that there appears to be a fire of some sort. Begin making your way off the path toward the glow and notice that it is a bush that is on fire, but that does not seem to be consumed. Feel free in your imagination to have whatever size or shape bush you wish, and let the fire burn however it seems best. As you make your way toward the bush, notice that you hear the crackling sounds of the flames. Notice also the warmth of the bush.

129

As you come closer to the bush, stoop down and take your sandals from your feet, for suddenly you have become aware that God is speaking to you from out of the bush and that you have been told that this is holy ground on which you are standing. This is the place where you are to meet the God of Abraham, Isaac and Jacob, the God of the oppressed.

As you proceed slowly toward the bush, which is burning but which is not consumed, be aware of the emotions which you are feeling. As you come closer to the bush, be aware that God is talking to you out of the flames which do not consume the bush.

You are now going to have a few moments alone with God at the burning bush. In this time you will discover the God who is near, the God who comes to his people. You will also hear God saying something to you about what it is that you need to do when you return to the world. Do not think now about the meaning of what God is saying to you. Perhaps it will come in words, or perhaps it will come in images or symbols which glow across your mind's eye. Again, do not think of the meaning now, but simply be aware that God is speaking to you, and enjoy if you will that conversation. Try to hear what it is that God has for you to do. Receive the commission which God has in store for you at this time, in the particular place where you live.

(Pause for four minutes)

Now it is time for you to begin to make your way back up to camp. Knowing that you can return to this place if you need to for further conversation and clarification, begin making your way back toward the path, stopping briefly on your way to pick up your sandals, slipping them on your feet if you wish.

You are now making your way back up the path toward the top of the hill. Be aware of the images and the words which you have heard and perhaps of the commission which God has given you, but do not yet try to analyze the meaning of that commission and its implications for you.

As you make your way back to the top of the hill, begin to come back now to the level of consciousness in which you are normally living. Be aware that you have taken an inner journey and talked with God, but that now you are coming back to the external world. Be aware of your body and of your surroundings. Come back at whatever pace seems best for your own experience.

DEBRIEFING

In the time that follows, allow those who wish to express themselves while just coming out of the meditation to do so. Be sensitive to the possibility that the conversation and sharing will sometimes begin without prodding or direction. Perhaps a question about the meditation may be all that is needed.

First ask about the experience in general. Ask if anyone wishes to share what kind of a visual experience they had. Then, after giving some short time to this, ask about the burning bush. Perhaps the members who wish to can share how they saw the bush and how they experienced God speaking to them at the bush. Ask what feelings or emotions accompanied the experience.

Now, if anyone wishes to do so, they can be given the opportunity to share the particular conversation they had and even the specific commission which they felt that God was giving to them. If the group has been together for some time, and if there is a sufficient level of trust in the group, perhaps there can follow conversation about the commission which has been received and the meaning of the experience.

Do not force the conversation and do not force anyone to share who does not wish to do so. You are striving for an atmosphere in which anyone who wishes may share. Since commissions from God may be personal, it may be that some or all of the persons in the group will not want to share what they have experienced. On the other hand, since commissions from God should be consistent with the received revelation in the community of faith, it is entirely appropriate for the group to wrestle with the meaning of any particular conversation. This is an opportunity for the group together to work in depth with the meaning of the Gospel in the world.

Meditation: Meeting God at the Cave

PURPOSE

To meet God, as Elijah did, at the cave and to discover that God comes in quiet, personal ways to persons and to receive a commission from God to go back into the world and to become involved in the world in a way that makes a difference.

BACKGROUND

The story of Elijah, prophet of Israel, takes place during the reign of Ahab, of whom it was said that "he did more that was wrong in the eyes of the LORD than all his predecessors." (I Kings 16:30) Ahab was a weak person who had his eyes on maintaining the powerful kingdom which his predecessor Omri had established. One way he sought to do this was by intermarrying with other powers, which brought him into an alliance with Sidon through his marrying of Jezebel, perhaps the most famous symbol of paganism in the Old Testament. In any event, Ahab did not have a particularly strong commitment to the God of Israel, and he did not prevent Jezebel's bringing into Israel her own worship of Baal, complete with hundreds of priests who would keep the cult in prominence. It seemed as though Baalism was in danger of taking over the place of Yahweh in Israel.

Into this situation came the enigmatic figure of Elijah, who represented the austere and pure form of Yahwism which had brought Israel out of Egypt and had put them in the land where they lived. Elijah called Israel back to Yahweh. He did so in a dramatic confrontation at Mt. Carmel where he proved to those watching that Yahweh was God and not Baal. The contest angered Jezebel who threatened the life of Elijah: "The gods do the same to me and more, unless by this time tomorrow I have taken your life as you took theirs." (I Kings 19:2) Elijah was afraid, and he ran for his life, running all the way to Mt. Horeb, the mount of God where, incidentally, Moses had also met God. While he was there, Elijah heard the voice of God come to him, and it is reported that Yahweh said, "What are you doing here, Elijah?" Elijah's feeble attempt to explain how he had justifiably run for his life was ignored by God. Elijah was told to go stand before the cave where he was hiding. There one of the dramatic scenes in the Bible took place. As recorded in I Kings 19, there came magnificent and dramatic cataclysms of nature, in none of which was found God:

> . . . a great and strong wind came rending mountains and shattering rocks before him, but the LORD was not in the wind; and after the wind there was an earthquake, but the LORD was not in the earthquake; and after the earthquake fire, but the LORD was not in the fire; and after the fire a low murmuring sound. When Elijah heard it, he muffled his face in his cloak and went out and stood at the entrance of the cave. Then there came a voice: "Why are you here, Elijah?" (I Kings 19:11-13)

God does not come to Elijah in the great manifestations of nature, but instead he comes to Elijah in a quiet, murmuring sound, in a voice. The God of Israel continues to come to human beings in a personal way. The God of Israel is a personal God. However much we might delight in the manifestations of the Divine in nature it is in the personal that God most truly and clearly comes to humans.

When God confronts Elijah, he clearly calls him to account for himself. "Why are you here, Elijah?" By implication God is expecting Elijah to be back in the thick of the battle in Israel, not hiding in a cave, feeling sorry for himself. Next, after calling Elijah to account for himself, God sends Elijah back into the fray, and he gives Elijah some interesting tasks to perform. One of the tasks is certainly a religious matter, the successor Elisha is to be anointed. Two other anointings are called for and they are surprising in their implication. Elijah is to anoint the future kings of Israel and of Syria, where Yahweh is not even recognized as God. It is a fascinating picture. The prophet of Yahweh is sent into an area where God is not known, and he is to become involved in a decisive way in the life of that country, indeed in the politics of that country. By anointing Hazael the next king of Syria, Elijah is participating in the downfall of the present king, Benhadad. Likewise, Elijah's anointing of Jehu as future king of Israel is going to contribute to one of the bloodiest revolutions in ancient Israel's history.

The picture is this: Elijah, avoiding his called-for involvement in Israel's society, meets God, who calls him to task for where he is and, in effect, for what he is and is not doing. Next God sends Elijah back into the world to become involved in the politics of that time. Once again, the encounter with God has led to the issuing of a commission to go into the world and to become involved in it.

PROCEDURE

After having the group read the appropriate passages in I Kings 16–19, and after describing the biblical and interpretive background above, have the group find their way into a quiet and comfortable position for the meditation. After the relaxation exercise, use either the following meditation or a variation of it.

THE MEDITATION

Imagine in your mind's eye that you are once again in the Sinai desert. You are dressed appropriately for the place and time. Feel that you are tired of your daily task and that you need to get "away from it all." As you see in your imagination now, there in the distance before you is a cave which simply seems to invite you into it for rest and escape from the pressures which are driving you. See the path leading up to the cave and begin making your way up to the entrance, noting the surroundings about you as you go in.

Enter into the cave a short distance. Find there a rock which seems to be comfortable enough and sit down on it. Now as you are sitting there, getting your breath, hear your name being called, and become aware that God is with you. The voice of God comes to you and asks, "What are you doing there?" At this point, make your way once again to the entrance of the cave and there note several dramatic natural events:

First there comes a strong wind.

(Pause ten seconds)

Next there is an earthquake.

(Pause ten seconds)

After the earthquake comes a great fire.

(Pause ten seconds)

After the fire there comes a quiet murmuring sound. It is the voice of God who comes again to you and has for you a commission to perform back in the world. Take a few minutes now to converse with the God who comes in the personal way to you and hear what the commission is which God has for you, a commission which is to involve you in the social and political world.

(Pause four minutes)

Now it is time for your conversation to come to a close. Not yet thinking about the significance of your conversation with God, and knowing that you can return here for further conversation if you choose, begin to make your way now away from the cave and back along the path toward the world. As you begin to leave the path, start coming back to your ordinary state of consciousness, the state wherein you normally function. Take your time and come back at your own pace.

DEBRIEFING

Let the opening question for the leader be a low key question that allows the group to respond as they see fit. Perhaps it will simply develop that no question is even necessary. After finding out how the meditation was experienced in terms of its imaginativeness and visualization, let the conversation turn toward the commission that God has given to the individual persons. Perhaps not everyone will want to share. This is the prerogative of any person. No person should be forced into revealing what could be a very personal experience. Nonetheless, allow whoever wishes to speak to share the insights which they have gained from the meditation.

If it happens that some have felt that the experience was not particularly fruitful, do not be alarmed. Not everyone will experience the meditations very clearly on every occasion. If the conversation with God was not finished, remind the participants that they can return into the unconscious to have the conversation with God on a later occasion. They do not need the group for the experience. It perhaps would be worthwhile for the group to share the different kinds of commissions which they perceive God issuing to them. Note that God comes to each individual in a personal and often unexpected way with a commission which is particularly suited for that person.

PART III
Resources

9

Christian Meditation in the Local Church

Christian meditation can be integrated into the programs and life of the individual Christian and the local church congregation. Christianity is a social activity. There is an obvious social dimension to the existence of the Body of Christ as found in the community of the faithful. Christian meditation therefore is appropriate for the worship and the educational functions of the church.

Christian Meditation and Worship

Both the individual and the corporate dimensions of worship can be enhanced by the practice of meditation.

The use of Christian meditation in the worship experience of the individual Christian is the more obvious. Combined with the study of the Scriptures, the singing of the psalms and hymns of the church, the vocal prayer life, meditation enhances the individual's daily worship experiences by adding variety and rhythm to the experience. Even more, meditation provides a vehicle for getting in touch with the Divine Presence.

For many it would be an added dimension that would make all the difference in the world in their perception and appropriation of Christian faith. This may not be necessarily true for every person. We are not all alike, but many will discover by means of Christian meditation the truth in the words of Thomas Kelly:

> Such practice of inward orientation, of inward worship and listening, is no mere counsel for special religious groups, for small religious orders, for special "interior souls," for monks retired in cloisters. This practice is the heart of religion. It is the secret, I am persuaded, of the inner life of the Master of Galilee. He expected this secret to be freshly discovered in everyone who would be his follower. It creates an amazing fellowship, the church catholic and invisible, institutes group living at a new level, a society grounded in reverence, history rooted in eternity, colonies of heaven.[1]

The individual Christian will find different times, places and occasions for the different types of meditation discussed in the chapters of this book. If Scripture reading is a part of the normal devotional life, then it would certainly make sense to include story meditations at that time. If a particular time in the morning and/or evening is set aside, then any combination or variety of the practices advocated are helpful. The individual Christian's creative testing of alternatives will provide what is helpful.

It is not necessary, however, to pack all the types of meditation into one experience every day. In fact, since worship should be a part of life and not divorced from it, it makes a lot of sense to allow the times during the day to call forth the right type of meditation. There need to be spaces in every person's day. Meditation is, in effect, "tailor-made" for those spaces.

Christian meditation can also be incorporated into group worship, both formally and informally. I would like to see more space and time created within the context of group worship services for meditation. Some churches have experimented with worship services in which there is a significant time set aside for the quiet searching for God, a time of listening.

The imaginative meditations offered in this book can also be adapted for group worship. So much of our public prayer is verbal and rationalistic, in essence a one-way conversation with God, largely constructed on the premise that God would not know what was going on if we did not keep him informed.

We should experiment more with group meditations, perhaps based on the Biblical readings for the day. It goes without saying that these should be led by a competent guide, but practice and sensitivity can provide that. This approach within the context of a formal worship can definitely enhance the group and personal experience.

The word worship originally was worthship. It is the act whereby we ascribe worth to something. Our commitments reveal the object of our worship. That to which we give ourselves is that which we worship. One purpose of worship is to call forth commitment from persons. Meditation can create the environment whereby persons can commit themselves by their involvement in the life of the Gospel. It is for this reason that Christian meditation should be considered much more for inclusion within worship.

Christian Meditation and the Educational Program

Christian meditation offers manifold possibilities for the educational program of the local church. Two directions seem to offer the most promise.

First, meditation can be incorporated into the life of existing study groups. In general, meditation should not be seen as an end in itself, but as a means to an end. Those groups in a local congregation that are gathered together for biblical and historical study can profit greatly from the added dimension that meditation provides. The use of story meditations can add to the reflective and thoughtful biblical study of such groups. In addition, there is the possibility of using the technique for the study of the history of Christianity. As a church historian I am particularly excited about this possibility and would like to see more churches using this approach. Perhaps it would begin to create the environment which would allow Christians to gain an appreciation for their common history.

A second use of meditation in the educational program is to provide the subject matter for one or more of those groups that the local church might design. I am particularly interested as an educator in the value of the short-term group in the life of the church. Although this is not the place to begin a discussion of that approach, I do want to say that I have seen this approach to be of value in this age of transience and change. Since meditation is a useful technique, the small group can be used to teach and practice this tool.

I have been a part of continuing small meditative prayer groups in the life of our church, First Community Church, in Columbus, and I can testify to the value of such groups. In addition, I have participated in short-term groups in a variety of settings, including Roman Catholic, Lutheran, United Methodist, and others, and I have seen how the short-term group also has value. If a church has chosen to utilize the small-group approach as a means of enhancing its ministry, I can think of no better addition to the program schedule than groups designed around the learning and practice of Christian meditation.

How to Lead a Meditation Group

The basic skills required for leading a meditation group in a local church are those skills required for effective small-group work in the first place, as well as a knowledge of Christian meditation as a tool in the Christian's basic repertoire of spiritual practices. It goes without saying that the leader of the group should be an experienced meditator, but group skills are as important if not more important. It is also crucial for the leader or guide to have a good grounding in the Christian faith and be able to articulate that faith. The experiences are not to be recreational but re-creational, and therefore it is important for the leader to be able to place the meditation and the comments afterwards within the context of the Christian faith.

Provisions should be made, therefore, to make it possible for group guides to be trained in meditation as a Christian discipline, in group leadership, and in principles of the Christian faith. The following chapter will recommend a few resources for individuals and potential leaders who want to read as widely as possible before leading a group.

It is essential in a group to create an atmosphere of acceptance and openness. There will be many different kinds of experiences which will be shared, and persons should know that their own experiences will not lead to rejection by the group.

It should be obvious that every group meeting should be carefully planned, even though opportunity should be left for spontaneity. The guide should plan the meditation which is to be used. He or she can either say the meditation by reading it, following notes, or from memory. A carefully modulated voice which can be heard by everyone should be used. The beginning guide should be careful not to read through the meditation too quickly. A slow deliberate expressive reading is better. Leave time for the individual members of the group to experience the meditation. Be careful to keep in touch with the group as to how the meditations are going. Perhaps the time being given is too long or too short. I have recommended four-minute pauses for the longer passive receptive meditations. Often this is too short, and five or six minutes is better. This depends upon the group. One warning is necessary. If the guide is not engaged in the meditation personally, the length of time will seem longer. Time sense is different in a meditative state of consciousness.

I have a particular concern also that leaders describe beforehand, at least in general, the meditation which is to be used. I suggest this because I have found that it allows the group to let go, trust the guide, and simply enjoy the experience. It also keeps guides from becoming too manipulative. It is tempting to work out meditations without thoughtful concern for what one is asking the individual members of the group to do. It is asking a great deal to expect group members consistently to put themselves in the hands of another for a trip into the unconscious. This type of trip should be taken with the utmost care for the individual members of the group, and therefore it is important to relate in advance the outline of the journey.

Some persons will often be concerned about the dangers of meditation. I think these concerns usually reflect the lack of familiarity with what an altered state of consciousness is. There is as little or much to be feared in the meditative state of consciousness as there is in going to sleep or in dreaming. As persons become more familiar with the practice of meditation they will find that communication with God is a friendly communication—one which inhibits rather than promotes the influence of the untoward forces which people fear.

A word of caution is not without some merit, however. If any person feels they ought not to participate in any particular meditation, they should feel no compulsion to continue. There is much in our unconscious which can be frightening. I personally feel it is better to come to terms with that dark side and to be aware of it, but a person generally knows what they can handle. If you or any person with whom you are working feels that they should not do any particular meditation for any reason, they should not do it and not attempt it until they feel comfortable in doing so.

When our group meets at our home for an evening of meditative prayer, we usually follow a fairly simple format. We spend the first half hour or so sharing what has happened to us in general and in meditation since our last meeting. Then I share as leader what reading I have been doing and make any suggestions for going in that direction. After mentioning the particular meditation we will be doing, we then experience the meditation. Afterward we spend from half an hour to an hour debriefing the meditation. Sometimes the time goes longer. These times together have been valuable times for us all and have provided the opportunity for spiritual growth and personal friendships. In the group the practice of the meditations has been a vehicle leading toward the greater goals of personal growth, spiritual insight, and personal interrelationships.

Usually the guide plans the meditation, but there have been those times when the group has taken the opportunity to plan a meditation on the spot. This is an interesting exercise which teaches the members of the group how to go about planning a meditation for themselves. On one occasion I asked the group at a workshop what kind of a meditation they would like to do next, and we set about to plan it. First, we started discussing various alternatives. One person mentioned the possibility of a biblical meditation. We talked about several different possibilities of that. One person was hanging back, and I asked him what kind of a meditation he wanted. It seemed he was looking for something more recreational or joyous. Another member of the group then suggested we might try to use the idea of a wind-surfer as a vehicle in the meditation itself. After trying to figure out how we would work that out, we all seemed to come to the conclusion that what we wanted was an opportunity to soar with joy, and that the particular meditation would have us walk to the top of a hill where we would then simply be lifted up and soar out over the countryside in an expression of joy. At that point we had created what would be an appropriate meditation, one in which we had all been present in the brainstorming. All that was left was for a guide to fashion the description, leaving the members adequate time to soar.

10
What to Read

When I began practicing the types of Christian meditation described in this book I discovered that although I knew a little about meditation in general and a little more about Christian mysticism because of my training as a church historian, there was so much more that I wanted to know. I began looking for anything and everything to read. As it happens there is not much available. There is much on one particular type of meditation, Transcendental Meditation, and there are a lot of books on Eastern thought and the esoteric world of the modern consciousness revolution. There is not very much for the Christian as such. Perhaps that is why so many Christians are somewhat reluctant to try meditating.

Consequently it seemed to me that one real service that I could perform, as a confessing Christian located somewhere near the middle of the road in modern Christianity, was to identify some of the writings that I have and have not found helpful. Although I do have some theological training, it might help you to know that I am a layperson and think of myself as such. I do take my Christian faith seriously and it is out of that context that I make the suggestions as to reading. If you have found the ideas in this book to be helpful, then perhaps you might find the judgments to be of some use in deciding what it is that you will want to read. The list is in no way complete. It represents only what I as one person have been able to investigate.

General Background Reading

Any person reading in depth in the area of meditation will eventually read in the area of transpersonal psychology, a relatively new discipline—at least newly named—which turns to looking at such matters as psychic research, the psychology of consciousness, and the psychologies of various religious practices. For the person interested in current research in these fields there are four journals, the *Journal of Parapsychology,* the *International Journal of Parapsychology,* the *Journal of Transpersonal Psychology* and the *Journal of Psychical Research.*

For a general overview of current work in psychic and ESP research, and recommended further readings I suggest the following books:

Lawrence LeShan, *The Medium, the Mystic and the Physicist: Toward a General-Theory of the Paranormal.* New York: Viking Press, 1974. Describes the research and conclusions of a clinical psychologist who has become one of the level-headed persons writing in the area of meditation.
Edgar D. Mitchell. *Psychic Exploration.* New York: Putnam, 1974. Edited by John White, this book contains a variety of articles related to current psychic research.
Sheila Ostrander and Lynn Schroeder, *Psychic Discoveries behind the Iron Curtain.* New York: Bantam Books, 1971. This book is a popular treatment by two journalists of the kinds of ESP and psychic research that is being done in the Soviet bloc of countries.
Montague Ullman, *et al. Dream Telepathy.* New York: Macmillan, 1973. Describes the research done in dream telepathy at the Moses Maimonides Medical Center in Brooklyn.

For a survey of the current consciousness revolution and some comments on a number of the offerings available from an insightful and humorous point of view I recommend:

Adam Smith, *Powers of Mind.* New York: Random House, 1975.

For a general analysis of the current spirituality with insightful and helpful critiques:

Theodore Roszak, *Unfinished Animal: The Aquarian Frontier and the Evolution of Consciousness.* New York: Harper & Row, 1975.

For some works in the area of transpersonal psychology and the nature of human consciousness the following are recommended:

William Glasser, *Positive Addiction.* New York: Harper & Row, 1976. The well-known author of *Reality Therapy* here spins out a theory that certain kinds of actions can lead to positive addictions, which strengthen persons as much as negative addictions destroy. He calls the state, which certain runners and meditators and a few others enter into as a result of their practice, the PA state; a book worth reading. If it was not written with tongue in cheek it would bear reading in such state.

Andrew Greeley, *Ecstasy: A Way of Knowing.* Englewood Cliffs, N.J.: Prentice-Hall, 1974. A study of mysticism and ectatic states, which suggests that more people than we know are mystics and are capable of ecstasy.

Abraham H. Maslow, *Religions, Values and Peak-Experiences.* Columbus, Ohio: Ohio State University Press, 1964. Written by the dominant figure in American humanistic psychology, this book suggests that religious experiences are natural experiences. An essential book for anyone interested in the nature of religious experiences.

Robert E. Ornstein, ed., *The Nature of Human Consciousness.* New York: Viking Press, 1974. A book of readings, which includes significant articles on consciousness and transpersonal psychology.

Robert E. Ornstein, *The Psychology of Consciousness.* New York: Penguin, 1975. A significant book, which relates current research in the field of the modes of human consciousness along with insightful reflections on the implications of the research for an understanding of human nature. If you read only one book in this area, let this be the one.

Charles T. Tart, ed., *Altered States of Consciousness*. New York: Anchor Books, 1972. A collection of articles on the variety and types of altered states.

Charles T. Tart, *States of Consciousness*. New York: Dutton, 1975. A significant work by one of America's leading researchers in the subject. Tart relates the status of current research and draws inferences from the research with interesting conclusions about human nature.

Charles T. Tart, ed., *Transpersonal Psychologies*. New York: Harper & Row, 1975. Includes an introduction on current research by Tart and several articles on religious psychologies by devotees of the various religions.

John White, ed., *The Highest State of Consciousness*. New York: Anchor Books, 1972. A book of readings by various authorities on altered states.

The study of altered states is often related to biofeedback work. The following two books provide an introduction to biofeedback:

Barbara Brown, *New Mind, New Body*. New York: Bantam Books, 1975. Very likely the best paperback book on the subject, but it is not easy to read.

Marvin Karlins and Lewis M. Andrews, *Biofeedback*. New York: Warner Books, 1975. A readable and more elementary introduction to biofeedback. It may tend to exaggerate the possibilities created by biofeedback. For some people biofeedback is a religion.

Relaxation is an integral part of meditation. The following two books discuss various approaches to *relaxation*:

C. Eugene Walker, *Learn to Relax: 13 Ways to Reduce Tension*. Englewood Cliffs, N.J.: Prentice-Hall, 1975. Written by a competent clinical psychologist, this book discusses ways to relax during the daily round, as well as offering some techniques that might be helpful for the meditator. Elementary.

John White and James Fadiman, eds., *Relax: How You Can Feel Better, Reduce Stress and Overcome Tension.* New York: Dell, 1976. An anthology of selected writings on relaxation. Interesting reading and includes a variety of helpful exercises.

Persons interested in the unconscious and in meditation may also be interested in watching for messages from their *dreams.* There are endless books on dreams and numerous theories about dreams. Most of these should be avoided. The following books are generally sensible in their approach and can be recommended as a starting place. Suggestions for further reading will be found in them.

Ann Faraday, *The Dream Game.* New York: Harper & Row, 1974; *Dream Power.* New York: Berkley Medallion Books, 1973. These two books are the place to begin. The author, an experienced dream researcher, is levelheaded and makes very useful and concrete suggestions about dreams, which really are helpful. If you read nothing else on dreams, read Ann Faraday's *Dream Power.*

Carl G. Jung, *Dreams.* Princeton: Princeton University Press, 1974; *Man and His Symbols.* New York: Dell, 1974. Although Jung is thought by many to be esoteric in his approaches, this pioneer of dream interpretation actually makes very sensible and straightforward suggestions about interpreting dreams. There are many writings available by Jung. These two will provide an introduction to his thought on this subject.

John Sanford, *Dreams: God's Forgotten Language.* New York: Lippincott, 1968. This book is an introduction to Jung's theories on dream interpretation by an outstanding Anglican theologian and dream interpreter.

Books on Meditation and Christian Spirituality

There are numerous works that can serve as an introduction to the field of *Christian devotion, spirituality,* and *mysticism.* The following are a few that I have found to be worthwhile:

Louis Bouyer, *Introduction to Spirituality*. Collegeville, Minn.: Liturgical Press, 1961. I have found this to be a useful introduction to Catholic spirituality and recommend it to the person whose knowledge is limited and who seeks an overview of the various aspects of the Catholic tradition. It is not without its biases, but in general these shortcomings are transparent. The historical sections are especially concise and helpful.

Aelred Graham, *Contemplative Christianity: An Approach to the Realities of Religion*. New York: The Seabury Press, 1974. This apology for the contemplative life by a Benedictine monk will be enjoyed by the person who has some theological training and wants an introduction to one lively tradition from within the Roman Catholic tradition. Graham denigrates history more than my historian's tastes prefer.

F. C. Happold, *Mysticism: A Study and an Anthology*. Baltimore: Penguin, 1970. I have found this book to be very helpful and useful. It is an introduction to the subject that I can unreservedly recommend.

Rudolf Otto, *The Idea of the Holy*. Baltimore: Penguin, 1959. This work is a classic study into the nature of religious experiencing. It is a difficult book to read but one that is well worth the effort.

Rudolf Otto, *Mysticism East and West*. New York: Macmillan, 1976. A comparative study of two major types of mysticism, focusing on similarities and differences.

Jean Leclercq. *The Love of Learning and the Desire for God*. New York: New American Library, 1962. An introductory study of monastic culture during the Middle Ages.

Chandler W. Sterling, *The Doors to Perception*. Philadelphia: Pilgrim Press, 1974. Written by the former Episcopal Bishop of Montana this book is a witty, thoughtful, and well-written introduction to Christian spirituality, which should appeal especially to Protestants who know only a little and want to know more. A book worth rereading.

Evelyn Underhill, *The Essentials of Mysticism*. New York: Dutton, 1960. One of the many books on mysticism by a leading English interpreter of that subject. This book provides a useful introduction to mysticism. One should also consult her classic, entitled simply *Mysticism*.

There are almost as many books on *meditation* as there are

meditators. The following books are from many different points of
view and are of varying significance:

Avery Brooke, *Doorway to Meditation*. Noroton, Connecticut: Vineyard
  Books, 1973. This is a delightful statement on meditation within the
  Judaeo-Christian tradition, accompanied by thoughtful line
  drawings.
Avery Brooke, *How to Meditate without Leaving the World*. Noroton,
  Connecticut: Vineyard Books, 1975. This book, a sequel to the above
  book, prescribes a certain approach to Christian meditation that
  might be used within group worship and study. Although it is
  somewhat limited in its understanding of what meditation is, the book
  would be a helpful supplement for use in the local church situation.
James Carroll, *Contemplation*. New York: Paulist Press, 1972. A short
  book containing four short articles on the contemplative vision. You
  will not learn much by reading this, but you may be stirred to
  thoughtful reflection on contemplation and the nature of the
  Christian's involvement in the world.
F. C. Happold, *The Journey Inwards*. Atlanta: John Knox Press, 1975.
  Although I generally enjoy the books by Happold, this little volume,
  which is a general introduction to contemplative meditation, will not
  appeal very widely to the average American. It is too British and tends
  to be too self-consciously literary. The exercises that are offered are
  too difficult for the average layperson to use. It is not, however, a bad
  book.
F. C. Happold, *Prayer and Meditation*. Baltimore: Penguin, 1971. This
  book is a useful study of prayer and meditation in various world
  religions and contains a selection of sample prayers, which enlarge the
  value of the book. A good introductory reference book for the layperson.
William Johnston, *Silent Music: The Science of Meditation*. New York:
  Harper & Row, 1974. This is a very popular introduction to the
  "science" of meditation offered by a Jesuit priest who has spent
  many years in Japan. Most of the problems I have with the book are
  due to the fact that Johnston and I have differing theological stand-
  points. A book worth reading.

Morton T. Kelsey, *The Other Side of Silence: A Guide to Christian Meditation.* New York: Paulist Press, 1976. A book designed for use by Christians practicing Christian meditation. It will be of limited value for the novice but should be of some use for the Christian who is looking for a guidebook that will challenge the mind and the soul. Kelsey is an Episcopalian priest who teaches at Notre Dame. In addition to his knowledge of theology he brings insights from Jungian psychology into his meditation approach. Of some value to the experienced meditator will be the section giving examples of several meditations. It is somewhat limited in its outlook in that it does not include discussions of mantra meditation and intercessory meditation.

Lawrence LeShan, *How to Meditate.* New York: Bantam Books, 1975. A brief introduction to the various kinds of meditation by a practicing psychotherapist. LeShan's approach is straightforward and levelheaded. It is not specifically Christian in its approach, but it is certainly worth reading by any Chrisitan meditator.

William McNamara, O.C.D. *The Human Adventure: Contemplation for Everyman.* New York: Doubleday Image Books, 1976. Written by one of the currently popular advocates of contemplation in the Roman Catholic Church, this book will be popular within that tradition, most probably among the clergy and theologically trained. Subtitle notwithstanding this is not a book for "everyman." I do not personally recommend it for the layperson.

Thomas Merton, *Contemplative Prayer.* New York: Doubleday Image Books, 1971. A very small but a very readable book on contemplative prayer by the best known of America's modern monks. It is primarily a theological reflection and not a guidebook or manual. It is worth reading.

Claudio Naranjo and Robert E. Ornstein, *On the Psychology of Meditation.* New York: Viking Press, 1974. A psychological study of the spirit and techniques of the various types of meditation. The book is worth reading since it is one of the few in existence that treat meditation from this angle, but it does not treat the subject as clearly as it might. The attempt by Naranjo to describe the various types of meditation flounders.

Herbert Slade, *Exploration into Contemplative Prayer.* New York: Paulist Press, 1975. This book, by an Anglican priest, will appeal to some theologically trained persons who want some theological reflection as well as some suggestions for practicing contemplative prayer. It will not appeal to the novice and probably not to the layperson.

Bradford Smith, *Meditation: The Inward Art.* New York: Lippincott, 1963. A "Quaker by convincement," Bradford Smith has presented a variety of meditative approaches, which will aid the person interested primarily in reflective meditation and quiet meditation. It is particularly good as it describes the art and practice of Quaker worship and meditation. Recommended.

Evelyn Underhill, *Practical Mysticism.* New York: Dutton, 1943. This book is not only an introduction to the world of the mystic, it also sets forth the stages of contemplative prayer. A book worth reading for the person who wants to go a little further than the level of mere introduction into meditation.

John White, ed., *What Is Meditation?* Garden City: Anchor Press, 1974. An anthology of various traditions on what meditation is. A useful but brief introduction to several different authorities.

Ardis Whitman, *Meditation: Journey to the Self.* New York: Simon & Schuster, 1976. A charming account of various systems of meditation by one who endeavored to experience as much as she could before writing. In essence, this is an apology for meditation from the point of view of a sympathetic journalist.

Jim Wilson, *First Steps in Meditation for Young People.* Greenwood, S.C.: Attic Press, 1961. A small booklet to be used with children eight years and older. It is more devotional in nature and will not challenge the imagination of children.

The following is not a book on meditation, but is a privately printed paper, which introduced me to the subject. I am looking forward to the appearance of the book by Bob Keck, but will mention the paper here in anticipation of the book's appearance.

L. Robert Keck, "An Introduction to Meditative Prayer and Its Application." Autumn 1974, privately printed at First Community Church, Columbus, Ohio.

Within the last year or so as TM grew so did the list of books on the subject. Few of the books are anything more than an apology for TM. Most of the books repeat what everyone has already long recognized—that practicing TM can be a physiologically and psychologically satisfying and beneficial experience. I am personally bothered by the package in which TM comes and feel that one need not pay to obtain a worthwhile mantra. I do admire the continuing education possibilities, which TM recognizes are important for its devotees. Among the many are the following:

Herbert Benson, *The Relaxation Response.* New York: Avon Books, 1976. If all you are interested in is the physiological/psychological benefits of TM, then this is the only book you will need. Understandably, since Benson's approach debunks much of the typical TM approach, it is considered anathema by the TM people and Benson himself is paraded as some sort of Dr. Jekyl and Mr. Hyde. All the more reason to read Benson.

Harold H. Bloomfield, et al., *TM* Discovering Inner Energy and Overcoming Stress.* New York: Delacorte Press, 1975. This is perhaps the best known of the TM books and can be recommended as an introduction to the many kinds of benefits that are available to the person who practices TM. Needless to say, it does not tell you how to do it.

Martin Ebon, ed., *TM: How to Find Peace of Mind through Meditation.* New York: New American Library, 1976. This book is actually on more than TM. There are some interesting chapters on different kinds of meditation.

Jack Forem, *Transcendental Meditation.* New York: Dutton, 1974. Written by the New York coordinator for TM's Student International Meditation Society this is one of the earlier descriptions of the value and nature of TM. Not a bad book, but not terribly exciting either.

Patricia Drake Hemingway, *The Transcendental Meditation Primer: How to Stop Tension and Start Living.* New York: Dell, 1976. Another of the many books written by a devotee. This one happened to be a journalist and she wrote a book about her's and others' experiences. If you like anecdotes, then read this one. The cover purports to tell you step by step how to do meditation. The only problem is that she fails to give you your personal mantra.

Una Kroll, *The Healing Potential of Transcendental Meditation*. Atlanta: John Knox Press, 1974. Written by an Anglican Christian who is also a physician, this book is an honest attempt to look at TM from the perspective of the confessing Christian. It is well worth reading if you are concerned about the implications of practicing TM as a Christian.

John White, *Everything You Want to Know about TM Including How to Do It*. New York: Pocket Books, 1976. This is not a particularly deep book and must have been written hastily. Nonetheless, it is an interesting and at time irreverent look at TM. Chapter five is an exclusive "how-to" lesson, which gives you a mantra. It is a book that can be used to balance the approach of the TM devotees.

The following books are not on meditation as such but are on subjects related to meditation.

Marianne S. Anderson and Louis M. Savary. *Passages: A Guide for Pilgrims of the Mind*. New York: Harper & Row, 1972. This book offers a variety of creative trances for persons wishing to explore a potpourri of mental trips.

J. M. Dechanet, *Christian Yoga*. New York: Harper & Row, 1972. The author, a Benedictine Monk, not only presents a fine discussion of Yoga and Christian Yoga, he also sets forth a series of Yoga programs to be followed by a Christian. This is an exceptionally helpful book for the person interested in Yoga from the Christian point of view.

Eric W. Hayden, *Everyday Yoga for Christians*. Valley Forge: Judson Press, 1972. This is a brief attempt at providing some Christian basis for practicing Yoga. It is not as successful as the book by Father Dechanet, but it is not a bad book.

Gay Hendricks and Russel Wills, *The Centering Book: Awareness Activities for Children, Parents, and Teachers*. Englewood Cliffs, N.J.: Prentice-Hall, 1975. This is a very useful book for the person who wants to practice imaginative meditations or who works with children in some capacity.

William Johnston, *Christian Zen*. New York: Harper & Row, 1971. An

earlier book by the author of *Silent Music,* this book reflects on the
relationship of Christianity and Zen and the ways in which
Christianity can develop a Christian type of Zen. It is a short book
and easy to read.

William Johnston, *The Still Point: Reflections on Zen and Christian
Mysticism.* New York: Fordham University Press, 1970. This book
contains writings on Zen and Christian mysticism by the above
author. He compares the principles and practices of the two approaches, with suggestions as to how Zen might influence Christianity
positively.

Robert Masters and Jean Houston, *Mind Games: The Guide to Inner
Space.* New York: Dell, 1972. This book contains a series of fantasy
and mind trances, which are for the advanced student and practitioner of such trips in the altered state of consciousness. The authors
are the husband and wife team that directs the New York-based
Foundation for Mind Research.

Buryl Payne. *Getting There without Drugs: Techniques and Theories for
the Expansion of Consciousness.* New York: Viking Press, 1973. A
series of exercises designed to assist a person "in his evolutionary or
spiritual growth toward enlightenment, Buddhahood, awakening,
satori, or whatever you choose to name it." These are not simple exercises and will require some commitment of time and effort to complete, but they do promise to enlarge one's awareness.

Related Reading in Christian Devotion and Spirituality

For the person who will be engaging in meditation regularly as a
spiritual discipline there will also be the desire to design a reading
program that will develop personal growth in *Christian spirituality
and devotion.* There are many books that can be suggested. I offer
the following as being among those I can recommend:

Anonymous, *The Cloud of Unknowing.* New York: Doubleday, Image
Books, 1973. This book has appeared in many editions. This particular edition is edited by William Johnston, author of *Silent Music*
and other books. This is a spiritual classic by a fourteenth-century

English monk and should be required reading for the person who meditates for some time and then wants to seek to find the Christian roots of his or her practice.

The Way of a Pilgrim. Translated by R. M. French. New York: Ballantine Books, 1974. This classic from the nineteenth century relates the story of the pilgrim who travels across Russia saying the Jesus prayer. It is essentially an apology for Hesychasm, but should be read by the person interested in prayer without ceasing.

Murray Bodo, *Francis: The Journey and the Dream.* Cincinnati: St. Anthony Messenger Press, 1972. There are many books on Francis of Assisi. This one by a contemporary Franciscan is a favorite among Franciscans.

Carlo Carretto, *Letters from the Desert.* New York: Orbis, 1974. Brother Carlo of the Little Brothers of Charles de Foucauld finds the source of his prayer in the Sahara and the solitude that it brings. This book was an international best seller in religious circles and is well worth reading for an introduction to contemporary spirituality.

Annie Dillard, *Pilgrim at Tinker Creek.* New York: Bantam Books, 1975. This book was recommended by a Franciscan friend, who said that anyone who wants to know anything about meditation should read it. If meditation is indeed a "different way of seeing," then this is one of the books to read. Best read in small snatches, it is a journal the author kept as she lived alone in the Tinker Creek area of Western Virginia. Recommended highly.

Fynn, *Mister God, This Is Anna.* New York: Holt, Rinehart and Winston, 1975. The story of five-to-seven-year-old Anna, as related by "Fynn" thirty years after. It is an enchanting and thought-provoking story. A true story worth reading.

E. Glenn Hinson, *A Serious Call to a Contemplative Life-Style.* Philadelphia: Westminster Press, 1974. This book reads like several sermons or class lectures and will not be too helpful to the person who is beyond the introductory phase of Christian meditation. Not a bad book but not outstanding.

Thomas R. Kelly. *A Testament of Devotion.* New York: Harper & Row, 1941. If I had only one book in Protestant spirituality to recommend it would be this book by the Quaker Thomas Kelly. It is already a classic and is worth rereading.

John Killinger, *Bread for the Wilderness, Wine for the Journey*. Waco: Word Books, 1976. This book is worth reading if only for the title and the style of writing. In fact, there is much more of value in the volume. Killinger has been coming to this stage in his own personal development for years and he writes about "the miracle of prayer and meditation" with passion and clarity.

Samuel H. Miller, *The Life of the Soul*. Waco: Word Books, 1951. A reprint of a classic work by the former dean of Harvard Divinity School. Recommended.

Henri J. M. Nouwen, *The Genesee Diary: Report from a Trappist Monastery*. New York: Doubleday, 1976. This journal kept by the Yale Divinity School professor while he was on sabbatical will serve several purposes: It is a good example of the value of journal keeping and it will provide some insights into life in a Trappist monastery. I confess I am still bothered by Nouwen's temporary residence. Your outlook has to be different if you know the sojourn will not last. A valuable book, nonetheless, but must be read with imagination and a somewhat critical eye.

Henri J. M. Nouwen, *Reaching Out: The Three Movements of the Spiritual Life*. New York: Doubleday, 1975. I personally recommend this book highly for its reflections on the nature of the spiritual life. I like Nouwen's style and appreciate what he says.

Elizabeth O'Connor, *Search for Silence*. Waco: Word Books, 1972. There are many O'Connor books worth reading. This particular one is planned for the devotional life, particularly of the person who intends to integrate meditation and contemplation into his or her practice.

Ruth Carter Stapleton, *The Gift of Inner Healing*. Waco: Word Books, 1976. This book relates the power of the visual capacity of the mind for engaging in the healing process by encountering Jesus at the point at which one is hurting the most. I personally feel that much more work and reflection needs to be done on the process that is used here and urge caution on those who would intend to use the procedure. I would guess that a fair amount of training and sensitivity would be necessary for a person to use the procedure without doing violence to the integrity of persons. An interesting book but not for everyone.

There are many *prayer books* available. I mention only the following:

Peter Coughlan, et al., *A Christian's Prayer Book: Psalms, Poems and Prayers for the Church's Year*. Chicago: Franciscan Herald Press, n.d. This collection will be useful for the person who wishes an aid for regular prayer during the day and throughout the year.

Michel Quoist, *Prayers*. New York: Sheed & Ward, 1963. I wish there were more books like this one. The written prayers in this volume are without parallel in my own experience. They are valuable for personal devotion and for public worship. They can be used over and over again and each time they become the prayer of the person praying. Highly recommended.

Notes

Part I

CHAPTER 1

1. Alvin Toffler, *Future Shock* (New York: Bantam Books, 1974), p. 45.
2. *Ibid.,* p. 326.
3. *Ibid.*
4. Anton C. Zijderveld, *The Abstract Society* (Garden City: Doubleday, 1970), p. 100.
5. John V. Taylor, *Enough Is Enough* (Naperville, Ill.: SCM Book Club, 1975), p. 27.
6. Saul Bellow, *Herzog* (New York: Fawcett World Library, 1965), p. 353.
7. Charles G. Finney, *The Circus of Dr. Lao* (New York: Viking Press, 1935), pp. 84-85.
8. George C. Bedell, Leon Sandon, Jr., and Charles T. Wellborn, *Religion in America* (New York: Macmillan, 1975), p. 485.
9. Kenneth Woodward et al., "Getting Your Head Together," *Newsweek,* September 6, 1976, p. 57.
10. Theodore Roszak, *Unfinished Animal* (New York: Harper & Row, 1975), p. 3.

CHAPTER 2

1. Robert E. Ornstein, *The Psychology of Consciousness* (Baltimore: Penguin, 1975), pp. 65-109.
2. Roszak, *Unfinished Animal,* pp. 53-55.

161

3. Charles T. Tart, *States of Consciousness* (New York: E.P. Dutton, 1975), p. 54.

4. See Karl Pribam, "The Neurophysiology of Our Remembering," *Scientific American*, January 1969, pp. 73–86.

5. In addition to Tart, *States of Consciousness*, see John White, ed., *The Highest State of Consciousness* (New York: Anchor Books, 1972) and Charles T. Tart, ed., *Altered States of Consciousness* (New York: Anchor Books, 1972).

6. See Stanley Krippner, "Altered States of Consciousness," in John White, *Highest State*, pp. 1–5.

7. Krippner, "Altered States," p. 1.

8. Thomas R. Kelly, *A Testament of Devotion* (New York: Harper & Row, 1941), pp. 29–31.

9. Tart, *States*, pp. 70–87.

10. *Ibid.*, p. 82.

11. *Ibid.*, p. 83.

12. Ornstein, *Consciousness*, p. 125.

13. For further comments on the psychological state of this kind of meditation, see Ornstein, *Consciousness*, pp. 140ff.

14. Ornstein, *Consciousness*, pp. 144–157.

CHAPTER 3

1. For a more complete discussion, see Louis Bouyer, *Introduction to Spirituality* (Collegeville, Minn.: Liturgical Press, 1961), pp. 68–104; A. Tanquerey, *The Spiritual Life* (New York: Desclee, 1956); Jean Cautier, ed., *Some Schools of Catholic Spirituality* (New York: Desclee, 1959).

2. John Killenger, *Bread for the Wilderness, Wine for the Journey* (Waco: Word Books, 1976), p. 40.

3. Killenger, *Bread*, p. 41. I am indebted to John Killenger for the gathering of meditative experiences in the New Testament. See pp. 40–51.

4. Bouyer, *Spirituality*, p. 76.

5. *Ibid.*, p. 79.

6. F. C. Happold, *Prayer and Meditation* (Baltimore: Penguin, 1971), p. 82.

7. Peter of Alcantara, *Treatise on Prayer & Meditation* (Westminster, Md.: The Newman Press, 1949), pp. 89–90.

8. Anthony Mottola, trans., *The Spiritual Exercises of St. Ignatius* (New York: Doubleday Image Books, 1964). The tradition is older than Ignatius, however. See Godfrey O'Donnell, "Contemplation," *The Way,* supplement no. 27, Spring 1976, pp. 27–34.

9. Alcantara, *Meditation,* p. 90.

10. Bouyer, *Spirituality,* p. 74.

11. Morton T. Kelsey, *The Other Side of Silence* (New York: Paulist Press, 1976), p. 215.

12. Fynn, *Mister God, This is Anna* (New York: Holt, Rinehart & Winston, 1974), p. 51.

Part II

CHAPTER 4

1. Adam Smith, *Powers of Mind* (New York: Random House, 1975), p. 126.

2. See John R. Dilley, "TM Comes to the Heartland of the Midwest," *Christian Century,* December 10, 1975, pp. 1129–1132. A Contrary Assessment of TM is given in the same issue by George E. Lamore, Jr., "The Secular Selling of Religion," pp. 1133–1137.

3. Una Kroll, *The Healing Potential of Transcendental Meditation* (Atlanta: John Knox Press, 1974).

4. See the article by Dilley and almost any book on TM.

5. Herbert Benson, *The Relaxation Response* (New York: Avon Books, 1976).

6. Benson, *Relaxation,* p. 83ff.

7. *Ibid.* p. 23.

8. *Ibid.* pp. 25–26.

9. *Ibid.* p. 159.

10. *Ibid.* p. 160.

11. John White, *Everything You Want to Know about TM Including How to Do It* (New York: Pocket Books, 1976).

12. Happold, *Prayer,* p. 127.

13. Anonymous, *The Cloud of Unknowing,* Edited by William Johnston (New York: Doubleday Image Books, 1973), p. 56.
14. *Ibid.* p. 95.
15. *Ibid.* p. 91.
16. R. M. French, trans., *The Way of a Pilgrim,* (New York: Ballantine Books, 1974).
17. *Ibid.* p. 12.
18. *Ibid.* pp. 12–13.
19. Carlo Carretto, *Letters from the Desert* (Maryknoll, New York: Orbis Books, 1972), p. 43.
20. *Ibid.* p. 46.
21. *Ibid.* p. 47.
22. *Ibid.* p. 50–51.

CHAPTER 5

1. Michel Quoist, *Prayers* (New York: Sheed and Ward, 1963), p. 19.
2. Samuel H. Miller, *The Life of the Soul* (Waco: Word Books, 1951), p. 68.
3. E. Allison Peers, ed., *The Complete Works of Saint Teresa of Jesus, vol. I: Life* (New York: Sheed & Ward, 1946), p. 79.
4. Kelly, *Testament,* p. 29.
5. William Johnston, *Christian Zen* (New York: Harper & Row, 1974), p. 40.
6. Evelyn Underhill, *Practical Mysticism* (New York: E. P. Dutton, 1915), p. 120.
7. Thomas Merton, *Contemplative Prayer* (New York: Doubleday, Image, 1969), p. 90.
8. James Carroll, *Contemplation* (New York: Paulist Press, 1972), p. 78.
9. Dietrich Bonhoeffer, *The Way to Freedom* (New York: Harper & Row, 1966), p. 60.
10. See Ann Faraday, *Dream Power* (New York: Berkley Medallion, 1973) for suggestions on interpreting dreams and for recommended further reading.
11. Avery Brooke, *How to Meditate Without Leaving the World* (Noroton, Conn.: Vineyard Books, 1975).

12. Elizabeth O'Conner, *Search for Silence* (Waco: Word Books, 1972), pp. 151-2.

13. Annie Dillard, *Pilgrim at Tinker Creek* (New York: Bantam Books, 1975), p. 35.

14. John Calvin, *Institutes of the Christian Religion,* Translated by Ford Lewis Battles, edited by John T. McNeill, Volume XX of *The Library of Christian Classics* (Philadelphia: Westminster Press, 1960), p. 35.

15. Marianne S. Andersen and Louis M. Savary, *Passages: A Guide for Pilgrims of the Mind* (New York: Harper & Row, 1973), pp. 54-55.

16. Gay Hendricks and Russel Wills, *The Centering Book* (Englewood Cliffs, N.J.: Prentice-Hall, 1975), pp. 41-51.

CHAPTER 6

1. Stephen Crites, "The Narrative Quality of Experience," *Journal of the American Academy of Religion,* September 1971, pp. 291-311. Sallie McFague TeSelle, "Parable, Metaphor, and Theology," *Journal of the American Academy of Religion,* December 1974, pp. 630-645.

2. James B. Wiggins, ed., *Religion as Story* (New York: Harper & Row, 1975). James Wm. McClendon, Jr., *Biography as Theology* (Nashville: Abingdon Press, 1974). John Charles Cooper, *Fantasy and the Human Spirit* (New York: Seabury Press, 1975).

3. Michael Novak, *Ascent of the Mountain, Flight of the Dove* (New York: Harper & Row, 1971).

4. Ted L. Estess, "The Inenarrable Contraption: Reflections on the Metaphor of Story," *Journal of the American Academy of Religion,* September 1974, p. 415.

5. Sallie TeSelle, *Speaking in Parables* (Philadelphia: Fortress Press, 1975), pp. 138-39.

6. Crites, "Narrative," p. 297.

7. Novak, *Ascent,* p. 67.

8. A Hasidic tale retold by Gershom Scholem, *Major Trends in Jewish Mysticism* (New York: Schocken Books, 1961), pp. 349-350.

9. Marshall McLuhan, *Understanding Media: The Extensions of Man* (New York: McGraw-Hill, 1965), pp. 22–23.
10. Carroll, *Contemplation,* p. 73.

CHAPTER 7

1. Georgia Harkness, *Prayer and the Common Life* (Nashville: Abingdon Press, 1948), p. 74.
2. W. Norman Pittenger, *Trying to Be a Christian* (Philadelphia: United Church Press, 1972), p. 95.
3. Montague Ullman, Stanley Krippner with Alan Vaughan, *Dream Telepathy* (New York: Macmillan, 1973), p. 205.
4. Sheila Ostrander and Lynn Schroeder, *Psychic Discoveries Behind the Iron Curtain* (New York: Bantam Books, 1973), pp. 14–28.
5. Killenger, *Bread,* p. 126.
6. L. Robert Keck, "An Introduction to Meditative Prayer and Its Applications." Privately published paper, Autumn 1974, p. 34.
7. L. Robert Keck, "The Discipline of Prayer," *The Christian Ministry,* July 1976, pp. 16–17.
8. See C. Eugene Walker, *Learn to Relax: 13 Ways to Reduce Tension* (Englewood Cliffs, N.J.: Prentice-Hall, 1975), pp. 7–17, for a brief practical discussion of this procedure.
9. Ruth Carter Stapleton, *The Gift of Inner Healing* (Waco: Word Books, 1976).
10. See Marvin Karlins and Lewis M. Andrews, *Biofeedback* (New York: Warner Books, 1972), pp. 40–42.
11. Pittenger, *Christian,* p. 97.

CHAPTER 8

1. Karl Hertz, *Politics Is a Way of Helping People* (Minneapolis: Augsburg, 1974), p. 29.
2. Meister Eckhart, "Sermon on the Eternal Birth," *Late Medieval Mysticism*, Ray C. Petry, ed., vol. XIII, *The Library of Christian Classics* (Philadelphia: Westminster Press, 1957), p. 188.

3. Richard Rolle, "The Mending of Life," *Late Medieval Mysticism,* Ray C. Petry, vol. XIII, *The Library of Christian Classics* (Philadelphia: Westminster Press, 1957), p. 243.
4. *The Way of a Pilgrim,* p. 13.
5. Kelly, *Testament,* p. 74.
6. *Ibid.* p. 94.
7. James M. Gustafson, *The Church as Moral Decision-Maker* (Philadelphia: United Church Press, 1970), p. 102.
8. *Ibid.* p. 99. I am dependent on Gustafson's discussion of the role of the deputy.
9. *Ibid.* p. 99.
10. Murray Bodo, *Francis: The Journey and the Dream* (Cincinnati: St. Anthony Messenger Press, 1972), p. 21.
11. Carretto, *Letters,* pp. 74–75.
12. Carroll, *Contemplation,* p. 22.

Part III

CHAPTER 9

1. Kelly, *Testament,* pp. 32–33.

Index

A

Acts 10, 94–95
Acts 18:1–18, 91
Amos the Prophet, 116–118
Anderson, Marianne, 156
Awareness of Presence of God,
44

B

Beckett, Samuel, 81
Bellow, Saul, 8–9
Benson, Herbert, 39–42, 155
Biofeedback, 149
Bloomfield, Harold, 155
Bodo, Murray, 158
Bouyer, Louis, 26, 28, 151

Brain, left and right hemispheres
of, 15–16, 27, 87
Brooke, Avery, 64, 152
Brown, Barbara, 149
Burning Bush, 88–90, 116; medi-
tation on, 125–132

C

Carretto, Carlo, 47, 124, 158
Carroll, James, 63, 125, 152
Change, reactions to, 4–5; a
world of, 3–5
Christian meditation, *passim*,
history of, 24–29; and non-
Christian meditation, 23–24
Christian Responsibility for the
World, 120–122

171

Christian spirituality, 151, 157–160

Christian spirituality and action, 111–114

Church, local, 139–145

Cloud of Unknowing, the, 43, 157–158

Consciousness, Psychology of, 14–16, 148–149

Contemplation, 25–26, 44–45, 112–115, 152–154

Corinth, the Church at, 90–91

I Corinthians 12:3, 69

I Corinthians 13, 91

Consumption, age of, 7–8

Coughlan, Peter, 160

Educational program of church, 141–142

Elijah, 116, 132–136

Estess, Ted, 81

Evaluating insights received, 67–70

F

Faraday, Ann, 150

Fight-or-flight response, 40

Finney, Charles G., 9–10

Forem, Jack, 155

Francis of Assisi, 48, 123, 158

D

Dechanet, J. M., 156

Deuteronomy 13:1–4, 69

Deuteronomy 18:21–22, 68

Dialogue with God, 52–70; in the Bible, 53–56

Dillard, Annie, 64–65, 158

Dilley, John R., 37

Dreams, 150

G

Geller, Uri, 103–104

Genesis 2: 19–20, 100

Genesis 12:1–2, 89

God, views of, 25–26, 29–31, 52–56, 59–61, 63–64, 67, 98–99, 104

Glasser, William, 148

Graham, Aelred, 151

Graham, Billy, 125

Greely, Andrew, 148

Groups and meditation, 141–145

Guidelines for use of meditation, 70–71, 105, 107–109, 142–145

Gustafson, James, 118, 120–121

E

Early church, 25

Ebon, Martin, 155

H

Happold, F. C., 26, 151, 152
Hayden, Eric, 156
Healing, 100–101
Hertz, Karl, 112
Hesychasm, 45–47
Hinson, E. Glenn, 158
Houston, Jean, 157

I

Ignatius of Loyola, 27–28
Imaginative meditation, 26–29,
    58–61; samples of, 58–61
Incarnation, 61, 121
Intercessory meditation, 98–110
Intercessory prayer, 98–104
Isaiah 42:1, 119
Isaiah 42:6–7, 119–120
Isaiah 53:7–8, 121

J

Jeremiah 1:4–5, 54
Jeremiah 1:11–12, 55
Jeremiah 2:13, 55
Jeremiah 2:27, 28, 55
Jesus Prayer, the, 46–48
John 14:11–14, 101
Johnston, William, 152, 156–157
Jung, Carl G., 150

K

Kamensky, Yuri, 102
Karlins, Marvin, 149
Keck, L. Robert, *ix, xi,* 64,
    105–106, 154
Kelly, Thomas, 19–20, 62,
    115, 140, 158
Kelsey, Morton, 28, 153
Killenger, John, 25, 103–104,
    158
I Kings 16–19, 132–136
Krippner, Stanley, 19
Kroll, Una, 37, 156

L

Leclerq, Jean, 151
LeShan, Lawrence, 147, 153
Luke 4:21, 120
Luke 7:22–23, 122
Luke 10:38–42, 114
Luther, Martin, 123–124

M

McLuhan, Marshall, 85
Maharishi Mahesh Yogi, 35–37
Maimonides Medical Center,
    101, 147

Mantra meditation, 38–39, 41–42, 43–45; Christian mantras, 47–48; method of, 41–42, 44–45, 49–51
Mark 11:22–24, 104
Mary and Martha, 31, 114–116
Maslow, Abraham, 148
Masters, Robert, 157
Meaning, the search for, 8–10
Meditation, *passim*, benefits of, 22, 40–41, 48; books, 151–154; dialogical types, 57–61; types of, 13, 21–22, 25–29, 35ff
Meditation, definition of, 13, 23
Meditative State of Consciousness, 19–22
Meeting our prejudices, 94–97
Meister Eckhart, 112
Merton, Thomas, 62–63, 153
Methods of meditation, 62–65
Migraine headaches, 106–107
Miller, Samuel, 56, 159
Mister God, This Is Anna, 31, 158
Mitchell, Edgar, 147
Moses, story of, 87–90, 125–128
Mysticism, 112–114, 150–151

N

Naranjo, Claudio, 153
Nikolaiev, Karl, 102–103
Nouwen, Henri J. M., 159
Novak, Michael, 83–84

O

Occasions for meditation, 65–67
O'Conner, Elizabeth, 64, 159
Ornstein, Robert, 15, 21, 148–149, 153
Ostrander, Sheila, and Schroeder, Lynn, 102, 147
Otto, Rudolf, 151

P

Paradigms of Christian activity, 114–115, 120–125
Paul, the Apostle, a visit with, 90–94
Payne, Buryl, 157
Peter of Alcantara, 26–27
Philokalia, 45
Pittenger, Norman, 99, 108–109
Planning meditations, 145
Post-exilic Judaism, 118–120
Prayer, 98–101, 160
Prayer as two-way conversation, 30, 52–53
Prayer of silence, 61–63
Problem-solving, 14–15, 77
Psychic research, 101–104

Q

Quiet observation, 63–64
Quoist, Michel, 53, 160

R

Reading, Suggested, 147–160
Reality, perceptions of, 17–19
Reflective meditation, 26–27
Relaxation, 149–150; exercise, 72–74
Relaxation Response, The, 40–42
Rhythm of Christian life, 31
Rolle, Richard, 112
Roszak, Theodore, 11, 148

S

Sample meditations, 49–51, 71–79, 90–97, 109–110, 125–136; books, 156–157; Burning Bush, the, 125–132; debriefing of, 50–51, 76–77, 79, 93–94, 96–97, 110, 131–132, 136; friends in the meadow, 74–76; how to use, 70–71; intercessory meditation, 109–110; meeting God at the Cave, 132–136; meeting our prejudices, 94–97; prayer of the heart, 49–51; purpose of, 49, 71, 90, 94; visit with the Apostle Paul, 90–94; Walk through the Park, a, 78–79
Sanford, John, 150
Silentium mysticum, 62
Slade, Herbert, 154
Smith, Adam, 148

Smith, Bradford, 154
Social action, 111–114
Society, Abstract, 5–7; character of today's, 3–12
Soviet Union, 101–103
Spiritual Christians in a world of action, 123
Spiritual life and active life, 114–120
Stapleton, Ruth Carter, 106, 159
States of Consciousness, 16–22, 44–45; altered states, 18–19, 44; function of, 17; meditative states, 19–22, 44
Sterling, Chandler, 151
Story, and Christian faith, 83–87; cool medium, 85–87; importance of, 80–81; living our story, 81–83, 122; power of, 84
Story meditation, 80–97; samples of, 90–94, 94–97, 125–132, 132–136
Story theology, 80

T

Tart, Charles, 20, 149
Taylor, John, 7
Telepathy, 101–104, 147
Toffler, Alvin, 4, 5, 7
Teresa of Avila, 57
TeSelle, Sallie, 81
Theological underpinnings of meditation, 29–31

Index

Transcendental Meditation, 13,
21, 35–45; books, 155–156; a
Christian alternative, 42-51;
Christian responses to, 36–38;
and Herbert Benson, 41
Transpersonal psychology,
147–149

U

Ullman, Montague, 147
Unconscious, the human, 14–15
Underhill, Evelyn, 151, 154

V

Visualization, 27–29, 105–107

W

Waiting on the Lord, 61–65
Walker, C. Eugene, 149
Wallace, Keith, 40
Way of the Pilgrim, The, 45–47,
113, 158
White, John, 43, 147, 149, 150,
154
Whitman, Ardis, 154
Wilson, Jim, 154
Worship, 139–141

Z

Zijderveld, Anton, 6